Alkaline Recipe Megapack Collection:

Four Alkaline Cookbooks in One! Countless Amazing Recipes to Supercharge Your Health

DevelopedLife.com

Developed Life is a collection of authors and writers committed
wellness, healthy lifestyles, spirituality and other important concepts.

First Printing – 2016

Alkaline Recipe Megapack Collection:

Contents

Alkaline Recipe Megapack Collection:

Alkaline Recipe Megapack Collection:

Alkaline Recipe Megapack Collection:

Introduction

Thank you a lot for buying this book! I hope it will assist with your healthy lifestyle choices. After you've done trying out these delicious recipes, please remember that a review on Amazon would really help me to keep going with this.

Get My Books For Free!

If you bought this on Kindle for a couple of dollars (or on paperback for a few more) I greatly appreciate it. However, keep in mind you also have a chance to receive some of my products for free. This is by signing up to my mailing list. I will periodically run a free promotional tool, and I'll let my subscribers know whenever I do this.

In addition, everybody who signs up receives a FREE copy of my book: The 20 Most Deceptive Health Foods

The point of this book is to educate readers about what foods are actually healthy, and which ones are not.

It's a must-have to take with you to the grocery aisles…

You can join the exclusive mailing list right now at the following link:

http://www.developedlife.com/andreasilver.

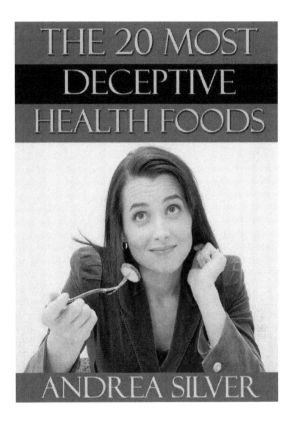

This is my completely free gift for my subscribers.

About the Alkaline Diet

There's a reason why both alkaline and vegan recipes are something to be very passionate about. In this section, I'm going to talk a bit about the importance of the alkaline diet, with some basic and essential information.

The Rise of Acidity

Western diets are very high in the acidic range. Some speculate that it could be one of the reasons that cancer is so prevalent in the 21st century. Regardless of whether this is true or not, we do know that an acidic body is not healthy.

One of the first things we need to do is identify what types of food to avoid due to high acidic content.

Alcohol

Although red wine is healthy for you in certain ways, all forms of alcohol should be taken in moderation, and one of many reasons is that they are high in acid content. Some wines have pH levels that approach 3.5. If alcohol is a regular part of your diet, you may be turning your body into an acidic nature.

Artificial Sweeteners

Aspartame, Sucralose etc are unanimously considered by most health experts to be deceptive wastes. Aside from other issues, including potential neurological problems caused by aspartame, these chemicals are also acidic in nature. Watch out!

Animal Meat

Going on an alkaline diet also means cutting out meat. Almost all animal proteins are acidic. The acidity is compounded when animal protein is fried in even more acidic oils or paired with white pastas.

Bananas

May be included in recipes as a tasty filler, but don't just snack on bananas by themselves, as they are high in acid content and relatively low in other nutrients compared to other fruits

Berries

Some berries tend to be more acidic in nature, such as raspberries and blueberries. Other fruits considered acidic are currents, plumes and prunes.

Black Tea

As with coffee, it's extremely acidic. If you love to drink black teas, make sure it's counter-balanced with plenty of alkalizing food.

Certain Nuts

Some nuts can be combined into alkaline recipes and it won't cause any harm. However, snacking on a lot of nuts—especially salty nuts— by themselves can lower your pH level. This includes cashews, peanuts, and almonds.

Chocolate

A hard one to give up. Chocolate is quite acidic. The cheap processed milk chocolates probably moreso than rawer dark chocolates and cacao. The best strategy for this one is to just keep the rest of your diet balanced to a higher level of alkalinity so you can still enjoy chocolate or include it in your recipes.

Coffee

OK, I know the media constantly shifts in-between coffee being good for you and coffee being bad for you. One week it cures cancer, the next week it causes heart disease. The truth is that coffee won't kill you, but it is very acidic. One cup won't be a big deal, but if it's part of your regular diet, it's a problem.

Cooking Oils

Common cooking oils (the cheap ones) like corn and sunflower tend to be quite acidic in nature.

Corn

Kind of an "empty" vegetable; high in starch and sugar and not much else. Corn is also acidic, so it would be wise to limit it, or cut it out entirely from your diet.

Most Dairy

One of the reasons vegan works well with alkaline is because it automatically excludes dairy. Most milk and cheese products range from either slightly acidic or neutral (cream, yogurt, etc) to highly acidic. As one example, parmesan cheese is much more acid forming than other cheeses with a very high acid renal load. In addition, American pasteurized cheeses usually have pH levels around 5— significantly more acidic than other cheeses. If a recipe listed does include cheese, like some of the Mexican recipes later, ensure it's not processed.

Processed Sugary Crap

Corn syrups, molasses, processed unnatural honey—these are all tickets to an acidic body. You have to start eliminating them ASAP.

Soft Drinks

There's 101 reasons to give up soft drinks (sodas). Yet another reason is because they are very acidic. If you are going into the alkaline diet, cut out soft drinks, carbonated syrup drinks, and any similar drink completely out of your diet. Coca Cola has a staggering pH level of 2. This stuff is pure acid!

Sodium

Aside from raising blood pressure, very salty foods also raise your acidity. Try to limit salt in your recipes and definitely don't sit around snacking on salty chips or nuts. On the same note, be careful of salty sauces and dressings. For an example, soy sauce.

Sweets and Desserts

Candy bars, caramel, junk food, you're asking for trouble! There are many reasons, from the saturated fat to the high fructose corn syrup, to avoid junk food. In addition, they are also very acidic.

White Bread and Most Grains

White bread actually has a pH of 5, which is very acidic. This also includes white pastas and other simple carbs. There are many other reasons to avoid these, as well—including weight gain, and how they spike your blood with sudden sugar rushes followed by those inevitable crashes where your energy levels drop. Subsequent sugar crashes also spike your hunger, making it a dieter's nightmare.

In addition to white bread, most grains in general are acidic, which is why a proper alkaline diet limits grains. However, you don't have to completely cut them out. Certain cereal grains, especially ones loaded with healthy nuts and seeds, can and should still be eaten.

Note that there's an entire line of thought that suggests we should cut out *all grains* from our diets. I don't really combine this philosophy into this cookbook because the alkaline diet is already 90% vegan, cutting out grains too would start to limit our food options too much for comfort. However, it *can* be done nutritiously if you are disciplined (please see my *Raw Food Diet* books).

White Processed Vinegar

Vinegar is supposed to be alkaline, however white processed cheap vinegars are quite acidic and should be avoided.

Other Sources:

Besides food, there are other ways to unintentionally acidify yourself.

One is through medications. Taking a lot of aspirin regularly will keep your pH low. This doesn't mean that you should forego aspirin, especially if it's part of a health curriculum to prevent heart problems, However, if your aspirin taking is optional, it might be best to eliminate it.

Tobacco is also acid forming. Smoking cigarettes has plenty of bad effects, least of all acidifying your body.

Exposure to certain chemicals, like herbicides, could also acidify you. However, there is a lack of research to cite in relation to this. (You probably shouldn't exposing yourself to *Round Up* anyways).

Debatable:

Some products are debatable about whether they are acidic or alkaline. For instance, mustard is often listed as both. As is vinegar.

Typically, the reasons for this include food processing or chemical additives that may turn something more acid. This is why white vinegar is more acidic compared to an organic brand of Balsamic or cider vinegar that could be alkaline. Another example is mustard.

Common store bought yellow mustard is going to be more acidic than some good horseradish or Djon mustard that will be fairly alkaline.

Balancing the Alkalinity

And now let's take a look at the types of food that will take a bite out of your body's high acid levels.

Alkaline Fruits

While some fruits are a bit acidic (tomatoes), others are very alkaline in nature. The ones to think about are: *mango, melons, papaya, cantaloupe, kiwi, apricots, apples, ripe bananas, dates, watermelons* and certain berries (acai is a good one).

A few of these fruits are especially noteworthy. For instance, a watermelon has a pH level of 9, and also acts as an excellent cleanser. You can further drink watermelon juice by itself as a thirst quencher which will also alkalize you.

"Acid" Fruit

When you think of alkalinity, do you think of limes and lemons? Conventional wisdom may suggest these are acidic, but no! They're "kings" of alkalinity. A lemon's pH level is massively alkaline at 9.0. Although lemon juice acts as an acidic compound, it's really electrolytic. Lemon juice can, for instance, balance out a person's pH level if suffering from heartburn from stomach acid. Consider keeping lemons on hand for most of the recipes in this book. If it works for that type of meal, sprinkle some lemon on it to further increase alkalinity levels.

Cinnamon

Cinnamon comes from the bark of the evergreen cinnamon tree. It has many purposes for flavoring, and it's one of the most alkaline spices. You'll find cinnamon included in many of the later recipes to provide kicks of alkalinity. In addition, as I talk about in my book *Natural*

Weight Loss Hacks and Secrets Revealed, cinnamon is an interesting ingredient because it's one of the foods that boosts your metabolism. A faster metabolism means the ability to lose pounds easily.

Coconut

You'll find coconut ingredients listed often as an all-purpose alkalizing treat. The best thing about coconut is its myriad of uses. The oil can be cooked with, the meat is a natural vegetarian source of protein, and the milk can be used in substitution of regular milk for vegan recipes.

Curry

Popular spice across Asia. Curry works in numerous dishes. You can buy it powdered and make specialty sauces.

Garlic

Very alkaline and very good for you for many other reasons. One of the best ways to enjoy garlic is to simply roast a clove in half in the oven at 400 F for 15-20 minutes. The caramelized garlic tastes sweet and can even be used as a spread.

Mushrooms

Mushrooms like Japanese Shiitake have been known to have an alkalizing effect.

Leafy Green Vegetables

One of the primary sources of alkalinity in this diet is going to come from leafy green veggies. The high level of alkalinity is the result of chlorophyll itself, which is an alkaline compound. The right "green stuff" in your diet also means an infusion of vitamins K, A, C, E, fiber, b2, magnesium, iron, folate, etc.

You should think about:

Asparagus: Named after asparagines, an amino acid that helps with brain function. This plant is unusually high in alkalinity.

Broccoli: Great tasting lightly boiled or raw. Highly alkaline.

Spinach: Easy to buy, great in tons of recipes. High amounts of every nutrient and also a good source of natural calcium.

Kale: A "superfood" that I talk about at length in my anti-aging and natural weight loss books. No matter what diet you choose, whether this or another one, stock up on kale and try to eat it every-day. That alone will make a massive difference.

Avocado: Nature's supply of healthy fats, alkalinity, and nutrients. Mash a single avocado and put some lemon on it for an easy to make and great little treat. You can also use it for some imaginative recipes. You can even include it in pies, mixed with pumpkin, for a green pumpkin pie!

Peppers

You will find that many alkaline recipes are loaded, when possible, with peppers. This ranges from chili peppers to more common (and perhaps easier to eat) bell peppers of various kinds; including the green, red, yellow, and orange varieties. There are more health benefits of peppers, as well. Red, yellow and orange bells are loaded with carotenoids which are important for skin health and have been known to lessen the advancement of age.

Sea Salt

Although sodium is acidic, this relates in part to the chemical processing that regular table salt undergoes. By contrast, natural sea salt is actually more alkaline. This is very good to know, as some food just doesn't taste that good unsalted—so you can replace your regular table salt and processed sodium products as appropriate. The best source of alkaline salt would be pink Himalyan rock salt which you can find at most specialty grocery stores.

Tempeh and Tofu (fermented)

These protein rich foods are standard fare in the East. As we are cutting out animal proteins in this diet, it's important to find appropriate substitutions, as every day you need to consume protein. While coconut meat is a good source, you need a variety—so I suggest to stock up at your local Asian grocer with fermented tofu. You can lightly fry tofu in some coconut oil for a tasty protein rich snack.

Tomatoes

Tomatoes are higher in acid content than most other fruits. This doesn't mean you cannot eat them. They should be included as part of a recipe with other alkaline foods. In other words, sprinkling some lemon juice on tomatoes is a nice alkaline snack. They alkalize in a similar way as lemons. Despite being "high acid" their pH levels are also very high, making them basic.

How to Create Your Alkaline Diet

Now that we understand the foods that promote or demote alkalinity, let's explore the fundamentals of how to prepare an alkaline diet for yourself.

60% - 40 % Rule

The guideline for an alkaline diet is to make sure 60% of the foods you eat fall into the alkaline list. This could be attributed to a single recipe, as well. So if you're preparing a meal of 60% green veggies and 40% red meat, it's still a dish that's more alkalizing than not.

Of course, to reap the benefits of an alkaline diet you should seek to increase the alkalinity ratio by a higher margin, especially at first. After maybe a month of making this more into a 90% - 10 % ratio, you can reintroduce more acidic foods into your diet. This is to give your body a stronger dose of alkalinity if you're recovering from years of overly acidic eating.

So, You Don't Have to Give Everything Up...

That's the good thing about alkaline diets is that you don't have to swear off your favorite foods forever. If you eat mostly alkaline foods all day, and then you have a white bread peanut butter and jelly sandwich—it's not going to kill you. The big picture is not individual meals but your overall dietary trends over the long-term.

Watch Out for the Major Acid Promoters

You need to be strict when it comes to the major culprits that have resulted in an overly-acidified culture.

The biggest culprit is coffee. This is surprisingly hard to kick, and you know something's not right in your body when you find yourself unable to give up any type of substance due to addiction. Sadly, caffeine is addictive, and if you guzzle six cups a day you'll find it's not easy to keep your hands off the espresso machine. In addition to coffee, black teas are also acidic.

The obvious solution to the coffee dilemma is green tea. Green teas often contain the caffeine you're craving, but without the acidic effects. In addition, the caffeine dose is milder so it's also a good way to kick your addiction to the heavier doses in regular coffees. Green tea is mildly alkaline in nature, and not acidic at all.

Some may be reading this and looking for the closest pitchfork—as they're that defensive about their coffee routine. Understand one thing: with the 60/40 rule, you can still drink coffee on an alkaline diet, *but you can't drink six cups a day*. You can drink two cups and ensure you have alkaline meals consistently.

The next major acid promoter is refined white sugar and junk foods of every variety. This includes foods like top ramen, which are highly refined and contain no nutritional benefits. It's important to work hard to eliminate these types of foods from your diet.

Next is tobacco. This is not a book about giving up smoking, and I've personally never smoked so I cannot offer much advice in this regard.

However, it's something you need to start seriously thinking about. While an alkaline diet may counter some of the acidifying effects of cigarette smoke, you're still handicapping yourself if you begin this diet without first giving up smoking.

The final major culprit are drugs. The USA is perhaps the most medicated culture in the world. Many pharmaceuticals are *highly* acidic in nature. When you are popping six or seven different tablets a day, it's a big problem.

Book One

Vegan Alkaline Diet Power Recipes

50 Alkaline Recipes to Energize Your Body, Stop Disease and Lose Weight – 100% Vegan

VEGAN
ALKALINE DIET
POWER
RECIPES

50 ALKALINE RECIPES TO ENERGIZE YOUR BODY, STOP DISEASE AND LOSE WEIGHT - 100% VEGAN.

ANDREA SILVER

How to Go Vegan

I'll admit, I'm not a strict vegan! However, I do go on vegan "phases". One of the major benefits of the vegan lifestyle is, in fact, the alkalinity levels.

However, this doesn't mean I can (or would want to) stay vegan forever. I still enjoy my fish and occasional dairy in moderation. However, it's definitely something to try out if you want to ensure you are eating in only the healthiest, freshest way possible.

It can be hard sometimes buying vegan food. A lot of specialty items I order direct from the company websites or from Amazon. Your local Whole Foods of course caters very well to vegan needs—but buying direct is a nice alternative sometimes because Whole Foods tends to put their prices way up.

With all that being said, let's now continue on to the recipes!

My Best Alkaline, Vegan Recipes

Creamy Pumpkin Soup

Mineral-rich, low-calorie alkaline diet soup for the weight conscious.

- 1 kg pumpkin
- 1.25 L alkaline water
- 30 mL heavy whipping cream
- 1 medium-sized potato
- 200 mL chopped onions
- 1 clove garlic (minced)
- 5 mL chopped parsley
- 1 pinch of cayenne pepper
- 5 mL salt
- 50 mL virgin olive oil

DIRECTIONS

- Cut the pumpkin and potatoes into small bits.
- Heat the olive oil in a saucpan and sauté the garlic and onion for 3 minutes.

- Add the water and boil the pumpkin and potatoes until they soften.
- Add whipping cream.
- Using a hand blender, puree the soup for 1 minute until it is creamy.
- Remove the heat.
- Season soup with salt and cayenne pepper and garnish with parsley.
- Makes 4 servings.

Spelt Berry Porridge

This makes for an amazing, nutritious breakfast.

- 250 mL water
- 250 mL coconut milk
- 250 mL thin spelt flakes
- 2.5 mL teaspoon cinnamon
- 10 mL maple syrup
- a handful of fresh raspberries, blue berries or strawberries
- a handful of almonds, pecans, walnut, hazelnut or any combination

DIRECTIONS
- Put water, coconut milk, spelt flakes, cinnamon and maple syrup in a pan and cook until it boils.
- Turn to low heat and stir consistently while allowing mixture to boil gently for about 5 minutes until it thickens.
- Ladle the mixture into a bowl and top with fresh berries and nuts.
- Serve and enjoy.

Tomato Phyllo Pizza With Basil

Crispy thin-crust pizza that makes a good appetizer when paired with a glass of wine, or with salad for a light supper.

- olive oil
- 8 phyllo sheets
- 120 mL thinly sliced onion
- 450 grams thin slices of tomatoes
- 4 mL dried dill weed
- 3 mL dried basil leaves
- salt and pepper

DIRECTIONS

- Add adequate amount of olive oil on pan by brushing to prevent phyllo sheets from sticking.
- Place each phyllo sheet individually on the pan, one over another, brushing each layer with olive oil before adding the next.
- Add onion over phyllo.
- Arrange slices of tomato on top.
- Sprinkle salt and pepper to taste.
- Sprinkle with dill weed and basil.
- Bake pizza at 375°F until phyllo browns, which takes around 15 minutes.
- Serve and enjoy.

Alkaline Tomato Salsa

A real tasty alkaline infusion. You can put this on many different recipes to alkalize them.

- ½ kg ripe tomatoes, diced
- 5 cloves of garlic, minced
- 250 mL of chopped fresh cilantro
- 1 red onion, finely chopped
- 1 small chipotle chile, finely chopped
- 5 mL adobo sauce
- 3 mL sugar
- lime juice
- salt, to taste
- black pepper, ground
- 0.25 mL cinnamon
- 0.25mL ground cumin

DIRECTIONS
- Mix the tomatoes, garlic and cilantro and puree the mixture in a blender until it smoothens.
- If a chunkier salsa is preferred, simply mix the ingredients without processing.
- Put the salsa in a larger bowl and add the onion, adobo sauce and sugar.
- Add lime juice, salt and black pepper to taste, along with cinnamon and cumin.
- Tastes best when fresh, but can be stored and chilled until

Quinoa Kale Rolls With Tomato Salsa

A dose of protein packed in a fully alkaline meal of kale, quinoa and tomatoes.

- 1 whole onion, minced
- 12 large kale leaves
- 400 mL quinoa (rinsed)
- 5 mL olive oil
- 500 mL of organic vegetable broth
- pinch of Himalayan crystal salt
- tomato salsa

DIRECTIONS

- Moderately pre-heat the olive oil in a saucepan.
- Saute onions for about 3 minutes, until it softens.
- Add the quinoa. Cook for 2 minutes, consistently stirring the mixture.
- Add the vegetable broth and increase the heat on the pan, allowing it to boil.
- Cover with a lid, return to low heat and let everything simmer for 15 minutes, until the liquid is absorbed.
- Allow the mixture to cool.
- Wash the kale leaves and trim the thick stems from the center of the leaves.
- Place 2 overlapping small leaves or 1 large leaf on top of a flat container.
- Add around 2 tablespoons of the quinoa filling mixture and spread it at the center.
- Fold in the leaf and roll it up to tip.
- Repeat the procedure for the remaining leaves.
- Serve the quinoa kale rolls and top it with the tomato-chipotle salsa (previous recipe).

Kale Salad With Brussels Sprouts

A must-try combination of two "super foods" that are very alkaline.

- 2 bunches of kale leaves
- 15 Brussels sprouts
- 100 mL raw almonds
- 30 mL pine nuts
- 30 mL pomegranate seeds
- Himalayan crystal salt
- ground black pepper

Dressing:

- 10 mL minced onion
- 3 small garlic cloves (minced)
- 30 mL Dijon mustard
- 75 mL fresh lemon juice
- 6 mL honey
- 60 mL olive oil
- 10 mint leaves, finely chopped

DIRECTIONS
- Prepare the salad dressing by putting all ingredients into a bowl with gentle mixing.
- Wash the kale leaves and remove the stems. Roll each leaves and cut finely to create long strips.
- Prepare the brussels by removing the thick bottom stalks. Slice in half and chop finely.
- Using a mortar or the flat side of the knife, pound the almonds to create smaller bits.
- Mix the kale leaves, Brussels sprouts and almonds into a bowl and add the pine nuts and pomegranate seeds.

- Gradually add the salad dressing until desired taste is achieved.

Avocado-Top Quinoa Salad

- 1 medium-sized cucumber, diced
- 1 avocado, remove seeds and cut in quarters
- 4 baby Roma tomatoes (seeded, finely chopped)
- 3 shallots or 1 red onion
- 250 grams quinoa
- 60 mL virgin olive oil
- 45 mL lemon juice
- 10 mL grated lemon zest
- a handful of fresh parsley (chopped)
- 45 mL pine nuts
- Himalayan crystal salt
- ground black pepper

DIRECTIONS
- Boil around 2 liters of salted water in a cooking pot and add the quinoa into the boiling water.
- Cover the pot, lower down heat, and simmer for 10-15 minutes until quinoa becomes tender.
- Preheat oven to 200°C. Evenly place the pine nuts on a tray and put it in an oven for 3 minutes or until it is lightly browned. Cool and place nuts in a serving bowl.
- Drain and rinse the quinoa under cool running water. Add the quinoa into the serving bowl and stir in the onion, cucumber, tomatoes and parsley.
- Add the olive oil, lemon zest and juice, season with salt and pepper and top with slices of avocado.

Romaine Lettuce Salad With Pepper Parmesan Dressing

- 2 romaine lettuces
- 2 radishes (chopped)
- 1/2 medium-sized cucumber (sliced)
- 1/2 medium-sized carrot (sliced lengthwise)
- 2 tomatoes (diced)
- 1 avocado (diced)

Dressing:

- 3 heaping tablespoons of egg-free (vegan) mayonnaise
- 1 lemon, zested and juiced
- 5 mL course ground black pepper
- 45 mL virgin olive oil
- 5 mL ground paprika
- 1 pinch salt

DIRECTIONS
- For the dressing, simply mix the mayonnaise, lemon zest, lemon juice and pepper. Whisk the creamy mixture while adding olive oil. Add the salt, stir until the mixture is consistent and set aside.
- Separate the leaves of the romaine lettuces and arrange in a wide bowl or plate.
- In a separate bowl, mix all the sliced ingredients of the salad.
- Stuff in the sliced ingredients into individual leaves of romaine lettuce and serve with pepper parmesan dressing.

Broccoli Garlic Quiche

- 180 mL egg-free substitute (powder)
- 350 mL almond milk
- 175 mL low-fat baking mix
- 5 mL salt
- 1 mL ground black pepper
- 1 mL cayenne pepper
- 2 cloves garlic, minced
- 575 grams chopped broccoli
- 1 medium-sized red pepper, chopped
- 1 medium-sized onion, chopped

DIRECTIONS
- Rinse broccoli in running water.
- Put half of the sliced broccoli into an 11x7 glass pan sprayed with cooking spray.
- Add half the onion and pepper on top
- Put remaining broccoli, onion and pepper over it.
- Mix egg powder, almond milk, baking mix, salt, pepper and garlic in a blender until smooth.
- Pour mixture over the broccoli in pan.
- Bake quiche at 380 degrees for 50 minutes or until lightly browned.
- Cool for at least 20 minutes and serve. Makes 6 slices.

Alkaline Parsley Gazpacho

Refreshing chilled soup made with more alkalizing ingredients.

- 5 middle-sized tomatoes
- 30 mL virgin olive oil
- 175 grams fresh parsley
- 2 ripe avocados
- 2 cloves diced garlic
- 2 limes, juiced
- 750 mL vegetable broth
- 1 middle sized cucumber
- 2 red onions, diced
- 5 mL dried oregano
- 7.5 mL paprika powder
- 2.5 mL cayenne pepper
- 5 mL dill weed
- salt and ground pepper to taste

DIRECTIONS

- Heat up olive oil in a pan and sauté onions and garlic for 3 to 5 minutes or until translucent. Allow to cool.
- Using a blender, puree a mixture of parsley, avocado, tomatoes, cucumber, lime juice, broth and onion-garlic mix until smooth.
- After blending, season the puree mixture with cayenne pepper, paprika powder, dill weed, oregano, salt and pepper.
- Blend the mixture again and set aside to cool in a fridge for around 2 hours.
- Remove from the fridge and serve. Makes 4 servings.

Pumpkin Ratatouille

The famous French "peasant dish" can be made with other ingredients, like pumpkin, to be extra alkaline and also uniquely flavorful.

- 500 grams fresh pumpkin, diced to bite size
- 250 grams tomatoes, diced
- 1 yellow bell pepper
- 1 red bell pepper
- 2 big onions, diced
- 2 big cloves of garlic, diced
- 5 mL thyme
- 5 mL basil
- 3 mL oregano
- 60 mL extra virgin oil
- 250 mL alkaline water
- a pinch of sea salt
- a pinch of pepper

DIRECTIONS
- In a pan, heat the olive oil and sauté the onions and the garlic for 2-3 minutes until translucent.
- Add the bell pepper and diced pumpkin and stir-fry for approximately 10 minutes.
- Pour in the water and add the tomatoes, bell pepper, thyme, basil and oregano.
- Stir the mixture well, allowing it to cook for a few more minutes until the vegetables are moderately tender.
- Makes for 4 servings.

Zucchini and Leek Fries

A great healthy side-dish or snack.

- 2 stalks leek, slivered
- 2 regular sized white onions, diced
- 1 zucchini, slivered
- 2 diced tomatoes
- 45 mL extra virgin olive oil
- 5 mL salt
- 5 mL crushed oregano
- 15 mL parsley
- 2.5 mL curry powder
- ground black pepper
- 125 mL alkaline water

DIRECTIONS

- Preheat olive oil for a couple of minutes in a saucepan and sauté the onions until brownish.
- Add zucchini and leek and stir fry for around 4 minutes.
- Add the water and cover the pan, turn to low heat and simmer for 8-10 minutes.
- Add the tomatoes into the pan, along with pepper and curry powder. Cover and cook for another 10 minutes.
- Before removing heat, season fries with salt and parsley.

Pizzoccheri With Broccoli and Bell Pepper

- 450 grams pizzoccheri (Italian buckwheat pasta)
- 120 mL extra virgin olive oil
- 2 cloves garlic, diced
- 1 white onion, cut in half rings
- 2 red bell pepper, cut in strips
- 180 grams chopped broccoli
- 3 tomatoes, diced
- 3 small carrots, sliced tinly
- 15 mL fresh lemon juice
- 5 grams oregano
- 5 mL yeast-free vegetable broth
- salt and fresh ground pepper

DIRECTIONS
- Boil around 2 liters of salted water and cook buckwheat pasta. In a separate pot, boil the broccoli in 1.2 liters of water sprinkled with salt and some pepper. Drain and set aside separately after boiling.
- Separately heat up half of the olive oil (30 mL) and sauté the onions and garlic until they become translucent. Remove heat and set aside mixture.
- Put the remaining olive oil in the same pan and add the carrots, bell pepper, and tomatoes. Cook until tender.
- Lower heat and add the broccoli, along with onions to the pan.
- Season mixture with lemon juice, oregano, vegetable broth and salt and pepper to taste. Remove heat afterwards.
- Stir well and spread over the cooked pizzoccheri pasta.
- Serve and enjoy.

Wild Pecan Rice With Broccoli and Greens

Another excellent side-dish that you can serve with a larger meal or in a potpourri.

- 150 grams wild pecan rice
- 75 grams shredded Nappa cabbage, finely chopped
- 60 grams Broccoli, chopped
- 175 grams young beans , chopped
- 2 carrots, finely chopped
- 250 mL bean sprouts
- 100 mL vegetable broth, yeast-free
- 1 chili pepper
- 1 fresh lime, juiced
- 50 grams chopped cilantro
- basil and Kosher salt to taste

DIRECTIONS
- Pre-heat the pan and begin adding the cabbage, broccoli, beans, carrots and bean sprouts. Pour in the vegetable broth and steam fry the mixture by constantly tossing it over flame. Set aside mixture.
- Separately cook the wild pecan rice by boiling it in water and some Kosher salt for 20 minutes.
- Mortar the cilantro and finely chop the chili pepper. Add lime juice until the mixture makes a good dressing.
- Place the rice on a plate, top with vegetable and lime and chili dressing.
- Sprinkle each serving with basil and some more salt to taste. Makes 4 servings.

Tofu Steak With Shiitakes

A hearty, vegan main-course that is also loaded with alkalinity.

- 450 grams firm slice of tofu
- 60 grams sliced shiitake mushrooms
- 40 grams grounded almonds
- 60 mL extra virgin olive oil
- half lemon, juiced
- 5 mL sea salt
- 2.5 mL black pepper
- 1 red bell pepper, julienne-cut
- 1 carrot, julienne-cut
- 3 garlic cloves, minced
- 10 mL honey
- 6 mL rice wine vinegar
- 30 mL soy sauce
- 100 mL yeast-free vegetable broth
- 3 mL cayenne pepper

DIRECTIONS

- Makes 3 steak-like, rectangular slices of tofu.
- Mix the grounded almonds, black pepper and half the salt in a small bowl.
- Soak each slices of tofu in lemon and dip into the almond coating.
- Heat half the olive oil in a pan and pan-fry the slices of tofu until they turn slightly brown. Put tofu slices in a plate and set aside.
- In a separate pan, heat half of the remaining olive oil over medium-high heat. Add the bell pepper, carrots and salt and sauté for around 3 minutes. Remove heat and set aside.

- Pour the remaining olive oil into the pan and add the garlic and mushrooms. Sauté for another 3 minutes and add soy sauce, vegetable broth, honey, vinegar and cayenne pepper.
- Lower heat and simmer for 3-5 minutes until mixture thickens. Remove heat and set aside.
- Serve tofu slices and top each serving with carrot mix and mushroom mix to your desired taste. Makes 3 servings.

Tomato Artichoke Spelt Pasta

- 200 grams spelt pasta
- 200 grams frozen artichoke hearts
- 150 grams fresh roma tomato, diced
- 1 medium-sized onion, minced
- 1 garlic clove, minced
- 30 grams pine fruits
- 5 mL vegetable broth
- 40 mL fresh basil, chopped
- 2.5 mL sea salt
- 2 mL cayenne pepper
- 30 mL extra virgin olive oil

DIRECTIONS
- Bring water to boil and cook pasta for 10-15 minutes or until tender. Remove heat and set aside.
- In a separate pot, cook the artichoke hearts in boiling water for around 30 minutes or until tender. Remove heat and set aside.
- In a pan, heat olive oil over medium-high heat and stir-fry onions and garlic for 2 minutes. Add the tomatoes and the cooked artichoke hearts and stir-fry for another 2 minutes.
- Dissolve the vegetable broth in 100 mL of water and pour into pan. Simmer over low heat for 2 more minutes with moderate stirring.
- Add the basil and season sauce with cayenne pepper and salt.
- Pour the tomato sauce mixture over the cooked pasta. Mix well and serve.

Alkaline Fruit Mix With Macadamia-Almond Cream

An alkaline dessert that is sure to please. If you're not strictly low-sugar, then go ahead and swap the Stevia with regular brown or granulated sugar.

- 425 grams macadamia nuts
- 75 grams almonds
- 650 mL fresh almond milk
- 25 mL vanilla powder
- 5 mL Stevia
- 250 grams fresh cherries
- 250 grams red currant
- 250 grams grape fruit
- 250 grams strawberries

DIRECTIONS
- Soak the Macadamia nuts and almonds in alkaline water for at least 10 hours.
- Drain the soaked nuts and put them in a blender. Pour in the almond milk and add the stevia and vanilla powder.
- Blend the mixture until a fine smooth texture is achieved.
- Slice the cherries, strawberries and red currant if desired.
- Remove the thick peel off the grapefruit, slice off the top cap and cut into sections.
- Mix all the fruits in a serving bowl and serve with macadamia-almond cream.

Jalapeño-Tomato Cucumber Smoothie

This is a very interesting recipe I make frequently that I didn't want to leave out. You might be wondering—how can jalapeno, tomato and cucumber work in a SMOOTHIE? The answer might surprise you. It's a bit of a more robust and flavorful version of V-8.

- 1 small cucumber
- 1 stalk of celery
- 4 roma tomatoes
- 1 whole lime, juiced
- 1/2 ripe jalapeño, finely chopped
- 2 basil leaves
- 1 pinch of pepper
- 1 pinch of sea salt
- alkaline ice cubes

DIRECTIONS
- Cut cucumber, celery and tomatoes into small cubes suitable for blending.
- Put the cut ingredients along with basil into a blender until a fine smooth texture is achieved.
- Halfway through the blending process, add lemon juice along with the finely chopped jalapeño.
- Season with salt and pepper and continue blending until mixture becomes consistent.
- Serve with ice cubes in 3-4 glasses.

Kohlrabi and Radish Carpaccio

- 50 mL extra virgin olive oil
- 1 kohlrabi, peeled & chopped finely
- 1 small radish, chopped finely
- 1 scallion, finely diced
- 1 celery root, peeled and finely diced
- ½ lemon, juiced
- 30 mL chopped fresh chives
- 30 mL finely chopped watercress
- salt and pepper to taste

DIRECTIONS
- In a bowl, mix the chopped celery and scallions.
- In a separate bowl, mix the lemon juice with salt, pepper, chives and watercress.
- Combine the lemon juice mix with celery and scallions.
- Arrange the slices of kohlrabi and radish on a big plate and pour the vegetable mix over them.
- Serve and enjoy. Makes 2 servings.

Kohlrabi Green Salad

- 3 green kohlrabi
- 1/2 small bunch cilantro
- 1 scallion, minced
- 60 mL broccoli spouts
- 30 mL extra virgin olive oil
- 15 mL honey
- 1/2 lime, juiced
- lime zest
- fresh ground black pepper
- Himalayan crystal salt

DIRECTIONS
- Prepare a dressing by mixing together the oil, honey, lime juice, salt, pepper and broccoli sprouts, along with the minced scallions.
- Peel the kohlrabis and make thin julienne-cut slices.
- Mix the kohlrabi with cilantro and lime zest and cover with the dressing.
- Serve and enjoy. Makes 2-3 servings.

Cucumber-Watercress Salad

One of the most refreshing alkaline salads I've made. I think you'll enjoy it.

- 1 bunch watercress
- 1 cucumber, peeled and diced
- 40 grams of freshly chopped parsley
- 15 mL apple cider vinegar
- 30 mL extra virgin olive oil
- 20 mL honey
- salt and pepper to taste

DIRECTIONS
- Prepare a dressing by mixing together the oil, honey, apple cider vinegar, salt and pepper.
- Rinse the watercress with clean water and remove thick portions of the stems.
- Mix together dices of cucumber, chopped parsley and watercress.
- Pour over the dressing of oil and honey.
- Serve and enjoy.

Lime Parsley Cauliflower Couscous

- 1 small cauliflower head
- 45 mL extra virgin olive oil
- zest of 1 whole lime
- 60 mL fresh chopped parsley
- salt
- pepper

DIRECTIONS
- Chop the cauliflower head and put the small florets in a food processor. Process until rice grain size is achieved. Set aside.
- Heat olive oil in a pan over medium-high heat for 2 minutes. Add cauliflower to the pan and cook for around 8 minutes with frequent stirring.
- Mix in the lemon zest, parsley and salt and continue cooking for 1 more minute.
- Remove heat and top couscous with some pepper.

Cauliflower Coconut Potage

- 450 grams cauliflower
- 300 mL fresh coconut milk
- 250 mL alkaline water
- 30 mL fresh lime juice
- 80 mL extra virgin oil
- 15 grams chopped cilantro
- pinch of salt and cayenne pepper
- 60 grams unsweetened coconut chips

DIRECTIONS
- Chop the cauliflower into smaller florets and steam for around 10 minutes.
- Put the cauliflower along with coconut milk and water in a food processor and puree until a smooth texture is achieved.
- Add fresh lime juice, salt and pepper, most of the chopped cilantro and the oil and mix until mixture becomes consistent.
- Pour into serving bowls and garnish with the remaining cilantro and coconut chips.

Strawberry Buckwheat Pancakes

Here's an example of a nutritious alkaline breakfast. Even something we traditionally think is less nutritious, like the pancake, can be turned into a healthful, alkaline power recipe!

- 1.25 kg whole-grain buckwheat flour
- 30 mL flax seeds
- 60 mL almonds
- 5 mL baking soda
- 150 mL egg-substitute (liquid)
- 5 mL stevia
- 130 grams strawberry
- 250 mL almond milk

DIRECTIONS
- Mix the flour, seeds, almonds, egg-substitute, baking soda, stevia and almond milk in a blender.
- Add some more almond milk as needed to achieve a thick, pourable texture.
- Pour mixture onto a griddle forming pancakes. Griddle on each side until it turns golden brown.
- Serve and top with strawberries.

Italian Garbanzo Beans With Asparagus

- 500 grams garbanzo beans (chick peas)
- 250 mL alkaline water
- 375 mL marinara sauce
- 30 grams fresh chopped parsley
- 20 grams fresh chopped basil
- 100 grams chopped asparagus
- 100 grams fresh chopped spinach
- 2 cloves of garlic, minced
- dash of oregano flakes
- salt and pepper to taste

DIRECTIONS
- Put the (drained) chick peas in a sauce pan.
- Pour in the alkaline water and bring to boil.
- Lower heat to medium and add the marinara sauce.
- Simmer for 1 minute before adding parsley, basil, asparagus, garlic, spinach and oregano flakes.
- Close the lid and simmer for 15 minutes or until the chick peas are soft for biting.
- Remove heat, put into a bowl, serve and enjoy.

Brown Basmati Rice With Lentils

- 120 grams sprouted lentils
- 950 mL water
- 2 chopped roma tomatoes
- 2 carrots, julienne-cut
- 2 stalks of celery, chopped
- 1/2 white onion, minced
- 2.5 grams cumin
- 2.5 grams basil flakes
- 2.5 grams cayenne pepper
- sea salt and pepper to taste
- 1 avocado, cut in quarters

DIRECTIONS
- Add a dash of sea salt to water and bring to boil.
- Add lentils, tomatoes, carrots, celery, and onion to the boiling water. Allow to boil for 2-3 minutes.
- Lower heat and add cumin, basil, cayenne, a dash of sea salt and pepper.
- Cover with lid and simmer for 40 minutes, occasionally stirred. Add more sea salt and pepper if desired. You can also add more of the listed seasonings if needed.
- Serve over brown basmati rice and garnish with avocado.

Spicy Guacamole Wraps

One of my favorite recipes, but I don't personally mind the heat. These taste fine wrapped in Romaine lettuce, but if you're not avoiding grains then some flour tortillas are fine, too.

- 2 ripe avocados
- 10 mL lemon juice
- 1 plum tomato, diced
- 1 small jalapeño
- 5 mL cumin
- 2.5 mL sea salt
- 1/2 white onion, minced
- 50 mL cilantro
- 70 grams Romaine lettuce, shredded
- 5 mL cayenne pepper

DIRECTIONS
- Mash the avocado flesh in a blender until desired consistency is reached.
- In a bowl, combine mashed avocado with chopped tomato, onions, lemon juice, jalapeño, cilantro, cumin, salt and cayenne pepper and mix well.
- Stuff portions of the mixture a single leaf or 2 overlapping leaves of Romaine lettuce and wrap.

Whole-Wheat Blueberry Muffins

- 300 grams whole wheat flour
- 7.5 mL baking powder
- 3 mL baking soda
- 30 mL honey
- 3 mL stevia extract
- 2 mL salt
- 250 mL egg substitute (try Ener-G Egg Replacer)
- 250 mL coconut milk
- 15 mL lemon juice extract
- 110 mL olive oil
- 1.75 kg blueberries
- 5 mL vanilla

DIRECTIONS
- Mix together flour, baking powder and baking soda in a large bowl.
- Mix the coconut milk and lemon juice in another bowl. Let it stand for 5 minutes and mix.
- In the same bowl, add the egg-substitute and olive oil. Clear the center of the dry mixture of flour and pour in the liquid ingredients. Mix thoroughly until the mixture becomes consistent and even
- Mix in the blueberries.
- Put mixture into muffin cups and bake at 400°F for 20-30 minutes until golden brown.
- Serve and enjoy. Makes 12 muffins.

Whole-Wheat Cinnamon Muffins

- 180 grams whole wheat flour
- 75 mL honey
- 10 mL baking powder
- 1.5 mL salt
- 2.5 mL grodund nutmeg powder
- 2.5 mL ground allspice
- 200 ml egg-substitute (liquid)
- 120 mL coconut milk
- 50 mL olive oil

TOPPING

- 50 mL honey
- 2.5 mL ground cinnamon
- 20 mL olive oil

DIRECTIONS

- Mix wheat flour, honey, baking powder, salt, nutmeg and allspice in a bowl.
- Add in the egg, coconut milk and olive oil.
- Stir mixture until moistened.
- Spoon batter into muffin cups greased with olive oil.
- Bake at 400°F for 20-30 minutes until golden brown.
- For topping, combine honey and olive oil, mix well, and add the cinnamon. Mix again.
- Drizzle mixture over the top of muffin. Makes 12 muffins.

Spicy Grilled Tacos

An alkalized Mexican feast.

- 2 sprouted wheat tortillas
- 30 grams tofu
- 130 grams chopped caabbage
- 1 small shallot
- 1 jalapeño pepper, quartered and seeded
- 125 mL chopped cherry tomatoes
- 1 sprig cilantro
- 1 avocado, peeled and cut in cubes
- 15 mL extra virgin olive oil
- 1/2 lemon, juiced
- salt and pepper to taste
- cayenne pepper
- 1 mL basil flakes
- 1 clove garlic, minced

DIRECTIONS
- Grill tofu in a griddle pan greased with olive oil. Add salt, pepper and squirt of lemon while grilling on medium heat. Season with cayenne pepper to taste, basil and garlic.
- To make the salsa, mix chopped tomatoes, jalapeño, onion and cilantro in a bowl. Add some salt, pepper and a squirt of lemon and mix thoroughly.
- Stuff tortillas with the shredded cabbage, shrimp, avocado and top with the salsa. Drizzle lemon juice over the top.
- Enjoy your spicy tofu tacos.

Spicy Mushroom Sausage

- 30 mL olive oil
- 250 mL chopped mushrooms
- 60 mL minced onions
- 1 garlic clove, minced
- 2 cups cooked black-eyes peas
- 15 mL tomato paste
- 60 mL nutritional yeast
- 125 mL whole wheat flour
- 15 mL finely ground chia seeds
- 50 mL water
- 45 mL vegan Worcestershire Sauce

SPICE MIX

- 7.5 mL garlic powder
- 7.5 mL crushed fennel
- 2.5 mL black pepper
- 5 mL salt
- 5 mL paprika
- 1/2 jalapeño, minced
- 2.5 mL red pepper flakes
- 5 mL oregano flakes
- 1 mL allspice

DIRECTIONS

- Combine all the ingredients of the spice mix in a bowl. Mix well and set aside
- In a pan, heat olive oil and sauté the onions, mushrooms and garlic until soft. Set aside to cool.
- Using a mortar, mash the black-eyed peas until completely crushed.
- Mix peas with tomato paste, nutritional yeast, spice mix and whole wheat flour in a bowl.

- Mix chia seeds with water until mixture is evenly dispersed and the seeds swell. Take 1 tablespoon or 15 mL of this mixture and add to pea mixture in the bowl.
- Add the mushrooms mixture into the bowl along with Worcestershire sauce. Mix well.
- Split mixture into 4 parts and shape each part into a sausage. Roll and wrap each of them in foil.
- Steam for 20-25 minutes and cool in a fridge.
- The sausages can stay there for weeks until use. Cook and serve topped with mustard, bell pepper and minced onions.

Vegan Sausage and Cabbage Soup

- 25 mL olive oil
- 350 grams spicy mushroom sausage
- ½ cabbage, sliced finely
- 1 whole spring onion, minced
- red pepper flakes to taste
- 5 mL salt
- 5 mL pepper
- 5 mL ground thyme
- 5 mL stevia
- 15 mL Worcestershire sauce
- 2 cloves garlic, minced
- 1 can of diced tomatoes
- 1.5 L water
- 1 cube chicken bouillon
- 75 grams white rice

DIRECTIONS
- Saute cabbage and onion in butter and olive oil in a saucepan over medium-high heat until onions turns translucent.
- Add the rest of the ingredients apart from rice, mix and bring mixture to boil.
- While boiling, lower heat to simmer and cover. Simmer until cabbage is tender enough.
- Add the rice and return heat to medium-high. Simmer without the lid until rice is cooked.

Alkaline Berry Sorbet

Another nutritious, fruity dessert.

- 80 grams unsweetened blueberries
- 40 grams fresh strawberries
- 1 banana, finely sliced
- 30 mL lime juice
- lime slices (optional)
- 60 mL soy milk
- 20 mL honey

DIRECTIONS
- Mix together the berries, slices of banana, lime juice and soy milk in a blender. Puree mixture until a fine smooth texture is achieved.
- Drizzle over honey and garnish with lime.
- Serve fresh and enjoy. Makes 4-8 servings.

Alkaline Cranberry Bean Soup

- 15 mL olive oil
- 8 cloves of garlic, minced
- 1 medium-sized yellow onion, chopped
- 500 grams chopped fresh kale
- 1 liter vegetable broth
- 40 grams cranberry (romano) beans
- 2(15 ounce) cans sliced carrots, undrained
- 6 Roma tomatoes, diced
- 2.5 mL basil
- 2.5 mL thyme
- 2.5 mL oregano flakes
- 2.5 mL rosemary
- salt and pepper
- 250 mL chopped parsley

DIRECTIONS
- Pre-heat olive oil in a saucepan.
- Mix in the garlic and onion. Sauté until soft and the onion is translucent.
- Rinse the kale without drying. Mix with the garlic in the pan and sauté, stirring, for about 15 minutes until wilted.
- Add 750 mL of the broth, 30 grams or 3/4 of the beans, all of the carrots, tomatoes, Italian herbs, salt and pepper and simmer for 5 minutes.
- Puree a mixture of the remaining beans and broth until smooth.
- Mix puree with the soup in the saucepan and simmer again for 12-15 minutes.
- Serve into bowls and garnish servings with parsley and parmesan and some pepper to taste. Makes 8 servings.

Lemon Cake With Almond Toppings

- 200 mL honey
- 1 mL stevia extract
- 50 mL olive oil
- 180 mL egg substitute (liquid, again you should try the Ener-G brand).
- 1 lime, juiced
- 320 mL whole wheat flour
- 12 mL baking powder
- blueberries
- almonds

DIRECTIONS
- Whisk eggs, add lime juice, flour, olive oil, honey and stevia extract.
- Pour mixture into greased and floured cake pan and bake at 350°F for 25-30 minutes.
- Garnish top with almonds. Slice, serve and enjoy!

Alka Lime Green Smoothie

Need something refreshing after a meal, or on-the-go? This sweetened smoothie is packed with energy.

- 1 whole lime, juiced
- 125 mL almond milks
- 3/4 cup crushed ice
- 30 mL honey
- 2.5 mL vanilla
- 1/2 banana
- 15 mL ground chia seeds

DIRECTIONS
- Mix all ingredients in a blender and puree until a soft, frothy texture is achieved.
- Pour into a glass and garnish with lime or any alkaline fruit.

Alkaline Blueberry-Banana Shake With Chia Seeds

- 100 grams fresh blueberries
- 1 banana, diced
- 15 mL lime juice
- 15 mL honey
- 100 mL almond milk
- 15 mL ground chia seeds
- 1 cup of crushed ice

DIRECTIONS
- In a blender, puree slices of banana with half the almond milk.
- Halfway through blending, add the blueberries, lime juice, honey, crushed ice, chia seeds and the remaining almond milk
- Blend until frothy and creamy.
- Serve with extra almond milk.

Broccoli-Watercress Salad

- 2 heads fresh broccoli, chopped to bite size
- 125 mL chopped red onion
- 2 bunches watercress, thick stems removed
- 25 mL apple cider vinegar
- 60 extra virgin olive oil
- 60 mL honey
- salt and pepper, to taste

DIRECTIONS
- Rinse broccoli and watercress in clean water. Remove thick portions of watercress stems.
- In a large bowl, thoroughly mix broccoli, onions, and watercress.
- In separate bowl, mix honey, olive and vinegar.
- Pour mixture over vegetable mix and toss to coat.
- Sprinkle with salt and pepper and serve. Makes 8-10 servings.

Spicy Fried Broccoli With Kale

- 1 bunch broccoli, chopped to bite size
- 1 bunch kale, stems removed and chopped
- 1 pinch rosemary
- 2 garlic cloves, minced
- 1/2 jalapeño or 1 red chili, deseeded and sliced
- 30 mL olive oil
- 100 mL breadcrumbs
- white pepper
- salt

DIRECTIONS
- In a pan, put olive oil in medium-high heat.
- Add garlic and rosemary and saute until scent becomes pungent.
- Add broccoli, along with 2 dashes of white pepper.
- Saute until broccoli is green and cooked.
- Pour in bread crumbs and continue sautéing until crumbs appear brownish.
- Add kale along with jalapeño or chili. Saute for another 3 minutes.
- Serve and enjoy!

Roasted Asparagus With Garlic

A simple and tasty side-dish (or main course).

- 450 grams asparagus
- olive oil
- 1 whole clove of garlic, diced.
- Kosher salt
- pepper

DIRECTIONS
- Rinse asparagus in water, drain and chop off tough edges.
- Completely coat asparagus by rolling them in a bowl with enough olive oil. Sprinkle with salt and pepper.
- Dice 1 whole clove of garlic into small pieces and mix with asparagus.
- Place asparagus in a baking pan and bake in an oven at 400°F for 25 minutes, until tender.
- Serve immediately.

Collard Greens With Kale

- 230 grams collard greens
- 230 grams kale, stems removed
- 1 spring onion, minced
- 2 roma tomatoes, chopped
- 3 garlic cloves, chopped
- 1 mL thyme
- 375 mL water
- 125 mL apple cider vinegar
- 10 mL Kosher salt
- Freshly ground black pepper
- 1 chili peper, chopped

DIRECTIONS
- Rinse collard greens and kale and chop into bite-sized pieces.
- Begin heating water in a saucepan over medium high heat.
- Gradually add remaining ingredients. Add the greens first.
- Boil mixture, stir occasionally, lower heat and simmer for about 30-45 minutes or until greens are cooked.
- Serve and enjoy! Makes 6-8 servings.

Iceberg Salad With Tomato French Dressing

- 1 head iceberg lettuce, core removed and chopped
- 4 radishes, chopped
- 4 spring onions, chopped
- 2 plum tomatoes, diced
- 1/3 seedless cucumber, chopped
- 1 cup shredded carrots, available in produce section

DRESSING

- 30 mL apple cider vinegar
- 45 mL honey
- 2 plum tomatoes, chopped
- 50 mL extra virgin olive oil
- 10 mL Worcestershire sauce
- 4 garlic cloves, minced
- Salt and white pepper

DIRECTIONS
- Mix iceberg lettuce with other chopped veggies in a salad bowl.
- In a blender, add all dressing ingredients except and process until mixture is consistent. Add a pinch of salt and a dash of pepper.
- Drizzle dressing mixture over salad. Sprinkle salt and pepper if desired.
- Serve and enjoy. Makes 6 servings.

Mandarin Greens and Almond Salad

- 1 small head romaine lettuce, chopped
- 1 small head iceberg lettuce, chopped
- 200 grams chopped celery
- 6 long stem green onions, finely chopped
- 2 cans mandarin orange, drained
- 1 cup sliced almonds
- 50 mL sugar

DRESSING

- 125 mL extra virgin olive oil
- 50 mL apple cider vinegar
- 80 mL honey
- 30 mL fresh parsley, finely chopped
- 5 mL salt
- 1 mL cayenne pepper

DIRECTIONS
- Mix together the lettuces in a bowl and set aside in a fridge.
- In a pan, mix almonds with sugar over medium-heat until sugar starts to caramelize and coat the almonds. Cool, break to smaller bits and set aside.
- To make dressing, simply mix all ingredients in a blender and process until completely mixed.
- Mix in celery, onions and orange in the lettuce bowl. Add the sugared almonds too.
- Pour dressing over salad and toss to coat.
- Serve fresh and enjoy!

Alkaline Avocado Quesadillas

- 2 plum tomatoes, seeded and cut in quarters
- 1 avocado, seeded and cut in quarters
- 20 mL chopped red onions
- 10 mL lemon juice extract
- 40 mL chopped fresh coriander
- 1.5 mL Tabasco sauce
- 24-inch whole wheat tortillas
- 15 mL olive oil
- salt and pepper

DIRECTIONS
- Combine the tomatoes, avocado, onion, lemon juice and Tabasco sauce in a bowl. Mix well.
- Sprinkle salt and pepper to taste.
- In a separate bowl, mix together coriander and some salt and pepper.
- Brush tortillas with olive oil and broil in a skillet until golden brown.
- Spread tomato-avocado mixture evenly over each tortilla.
- Cut quesadilla into 4 wedges.
- Serve warm and enjoy!

Spicy Spinach Quiche

- 15 mL olive oil
- 1 spring onion, chopped
- 350 grams spinach
- 2 plum tomatoes, chopped
- 1 mL cayenne pepper
- 1 clove garlic, minced
- 400mL liquid egg substitute (Ener-G)
- salt and pepper

DIRECTIONS
- Preheat oven to 350°F.
- Heat oil in a pan over medium-high heat. Add the onions and sauté for around 5 minutes or until browned.
- Add the spinach, cook until most of the liquid or moisture evaporates and set aside to cool.
- In a bowl, add egg substitute along with tomatoes, garlic and cayenne pepper.
- Thoroughly mix egg and spinach mixture and season with some salt and pepper
- Put mixture on a greased pie plate, evenly spread.
- Bake for 40-50 minutes in oven until top is turns brown.

Alkaline Spinach and Mushroom Soup

- 150 grams spinach
- 2 cups thinly sliced mushrooms
- 220 grams firm tofu, diced to bit size
- 1 liter vegetable broth
- 350 mL alkaline water
- 25 mL soy sauce
- 25 mL apple cider vinegar
- 15 mL olive oil
- 4 cloves garlic, minced
- 15 mL minced ginger
- 3 green onions, chopped

DIRECTIONS

- Combine broth, water, soy sauce, vinegar, olive oil, garlic and ginger in large saucepan and boil over medium-high heat.
- Add the chopped mushrooms and simmer for about 5 minutes until mushrooms are tender.
- Add tofu, spinach and green onions and simmer for 2-3 minutes until spinach wilts and tofu is heated enough.
- Ladle into serving bowls and season with salt and pepper to taste.

Quinoa Green Stir Fry

- 180 grams quinoa
- 500 mL alkaline water
- 30 mL extra virgin olive oil
- 1 clove garlic, minced
- 120 mL pecans
- 40 grams spinach leaves
- 250 mL cherry tomatoes
- fresh basil leaves

DIRECTIONS
- Rinse quinoa in a small bowl and drain.
- Heat olive oil in medium-sized pan., add quinoa and toast, stirring, over medium heat for about 10 minutes until golden brown.
- Add the minced garlic and cook for 1 more minute before adding salt and water. Bring to boil.
- Cover with lid, lower heat, cook for 15-20 minutes until water is absorbed.
- Meanwhile, spread pecans in a small pan and stir over medium-low heat for about 5 minutes until toasted and set aside.
- When quinoa is done, add the spinach and tomatoes to the pan. Stir fry over medium heat for around 1 minute until spinach is wilted.
- Stir in the toasted walnuts. Heat for 1 more minute.
- Garnish with basil and serve immediately.

Lime Basmati Rice With Garlic and Cilantro

- 5 mL olive oil
- 15 mL fresh cilantro leaves, chopped
- 1-2 cloves garlic, minced
- 1/2 spring onion or 1 shallot
- 150 grams basmati rice
- 300 mL water
- 2.5 mL salt
- 1 whole medium-sized lime

DIRECTIONS

- Heat olive oil in a saucepan over medium heat.
- Add in rice and lime juice and stir for 1 minute before adding salt and water.
- Increase heat and bring to boil.
- Cover and simmer over low heat for about 25 minutes until rice is cooked.
- Serve garnished with cilantro.

Roasted Garlic Brussels Sprouts

- 650 grams Brussels sprouts
- 45 mL olive oil
- 3 mL Kosher salt
- 2.5 mL ground black pepper
- 5 cloves garlic, minced

DIRECTIONS
- Preheat oven to 400°F.
- Cut off thick bottom stalks of Brussels sprouts and remove yellow leaves.
- In a low-heated pan, mix sprouts with olive oil, garlic and pepper and cook without stirring until sprouts begin to brown.
- Transfer to a baking pan and roast for 35 to 40 minutes, until crisp outside and soft inside.
- Shake pan occasionally to evenly brown the Brussels.
- Sprinkle with more salt if desired. Serve with vinegar.

Kale and Spinach Pesto

You can use this quick, super healthy sauce to coat just about any other recipe you can think of in-order to create an alkaline infusion.

- 350 mL chopped fresh kale
- 350 mL chopped spinach
- 125 mL chopped toasted almonds
- 3 garlic cloves, crushed
- 1/2 lemon, juiced
- 125 mL extra virgin olive oil
- salt and pepper

DIRECTIONS
- Bring a small pot of water to boil, blanch greens (kale and spinach) for 3 minutes and drain then set aside to cool.
- Place in a blender the almonds, garlic and lemon juice and process until well-mixed.
- Halfway, pour in the olive oil and continue blending until well blended and smooth. Season with some salt and pepper up to desired taste.
- Serve immediately with pasta or other alkaline dishes or keep in a fridge for up to 5 days.

That's it for now!

Healthy & Perfect Alkaline Smoothies

Liquid Alkaline Recipes for Weight Loss and Invigorating Health Effects – 100% Vegan

Healthy & Perfect
ALKALINE
SMOOTHIES

Liquid Alkaline Recipes for Weight Loss and Invigorating Health Effects - 100% Vegan

ANDREA SILVER

The Smoothie Angle

One of the major benefits of smoothies, and juicing, is that you're getting sizable RAW doses of high-quality fruits and veggies. Raw food is known to contain higher amounts of vitamins and nutrients compared to cooked alternatives. The second big advantage relates to speed and efficiency.

A major contributor to people being unable to maintain their diets relates to our busy schedules and fast-paced lives. The whole idea behind juicing and creating custom smoothies is to have efficient, healthy doses of nutritional ingredients. You can make one of these smoothie recipes in as little as a couple of minutes, and you can take it "on the go".

Some of the thicker smoothies, like the ones with avocado, coconut, kale, etc will also satiate hunger cravings. You can simply make a smoothie while you're heading out the door as your liquid breakfast, and you're guaranteed to lose weight so long as you stay moderately active the rest of the day.

One more factor to consider is saving money. If you're like me, you get a bit repulsed by franchises like "Jamba Juice" that charge outrageous amounts of money for their liquid snacks. The actual cost to throw some apple and carrot or cucumber in a blender or juicer is a few cents, but these guys will charge $5.00 or more.

These are all great reasons to start juicing, but what about the alkalinity factor? Here's the deal: these smoothies are more than just light-weight health snacks—the recipes outlined in this book are also designed around balancing your pH levels and eliminating acidity. This is pretty important if you want to:

- Increase your chances of successfully losing weight.
- Enhance your energy levels.
- Decrease the risk of many serious diseases, including cancer.

Most fruit and veggie rich smoothies are going to be alkalizing, but the ones I included are designed to optimize this factor. Ingredients like kale, spinach, avocado, and other veggies will do the job much faster than smoothies without the added greenery.

In addition, these recipes are vegan. There's an important reason for this: dairy is not alkalizing, and it will instead acidify you. A banana and peach smoothie full of milk isn't doing anything to help your alkalinity (or your waistline, or even sugar levels for that matter). Replace the milk with almond milk, on the other hand, and the health effects greatly increase.

Finally, keep these smoothies are also a great part of a detox regiment. This involves temporarily consuming nothing but liquid drinks as a way to 'flush' your body of toxins. There are many resources online, or through your dietitian, to help you do this. It may involve choosing a specific ingredient with cleansing effects, and adding it to each of the smoothies you make during the detox period. Detoxes have been known to fight diseases, treat or cure existing problems (such as parasites), and help with weight loss goals.

Now since you're well-educated on the nature of alkalinity, and smoothies in general, let's dive into my hand-picked recipes!

Healthy Alkaline Smoothie Recipes

Green Peach Smoothie

A great drink for peach lovers, and a tasty way to start the day.

- 1 ripe banana
- 1 ripe peach, pitted
- 1 cup of baby spinach leaves
- 1 teaspoon agave nectar
- 237 mL coconut milk

DIRECTIONS
- Place the banana, peach, spinach and agave nectar in a blender.
- Pour in the coconut milk and blend until smooth and creamy.
- Enjoy.

Servings: 1

Blueberry, Grape and Green Smoothie

Nutrient-rich spinach is hidden in this healthy green smoothie. Try it and get your daily dose of vitamins.

- 3 cups of romaine lettuce, torn
- 1 cup of spinach, torn
- Handful of blueberries
- Handful of grapes

DIRECTIONS
- Thoroughly wash the spinach, lettuce, and place in a blender.
- Throw in the grapes and blueberries, add about ¾ cup water and pulse for 30-40 seconds until smooth.

Servings: 1

Banana Kale Smoothie

Banana, kale and mint pair well in this heart healthy smoothie recipe. The little bit of cayenne pepper gives this a surprising 'kick'. Taste it and see what I mean.

- 1 organic kale leave, stem removed
- A dash of cayenne pepper
- 1-2 bananas
- A handful of ice
- 2-3 mint leaves

DIRECTIONS
- Place the kale, bananas, mint and ice in a blender, season with cayenne pepper and pulse for 25-35 seconds until smooth and creamy.
- Enjoy.

Servings: 1

Fresh Green Mint Smoothie

This is a great smoothie recipe that features pear, kale, mint and orange juice. Kale is a highly alkalizing superfood, along with the citrus.

- 1 ripe pear, cored, chopped
- 1 bunch of kale
- 3-4 mint leaves
- 237 mL purified water
- 237 mL fresh orange juice

DIRECTIONS
- Place the pear, kale and mint in a high speed blender.
- Pour in the water and orange juice and blend until smooth.
- Enjoy.

Servings: 1

Super Healthy Almond Avocado Smoothie

Another green smoothie packed with plenty of vitamins and nutrients.

- 1 avocado, peeled, pitted
- 237 mL raw almond milk
- 1 lemon juice
- 1/8 teaspoon cinnamon
- 2-3 leaves of kale
- 3-4 mint leaves
- 5-6 cucumber slices
- A pinch of cocoa powder

DIRECTIONS
- Place the avocado, lemon juice, cucumber, kale, mint, almond milk, cinnamon in a blender and pulse until smooth.
- Pour the mixture into a tall glass, sprinkle with a pinch of cocoa powder and enjoy.

Servings: 1

Coconut Grapefruit Smoothie

Try this energizing combination of grapefruit, spinach, coconut milk and agave nectar.

- Fresh juice of 1 grapefruit
- 237 mL coconut milk
- 1 cup spinach, washed, torn
- 2/3 teaspoon agave nectar

DIRECTIONS
- Add the spinach, grapefruit juice, agave nectar and coconut milk to a blender and pulse until smooth.
- Enjoy.

Servings: 1

Vegetable Power Smoothie

A filling and healthy savory smoothie that can be served as a breakfast or a light lunch. As an optional ingredient, try a bunch of Tabasco hot sauce.

- 1 cucumber, peeled, quartered
- 4 tomatoes, peeled, halved
- 1 garlic clove
- ½ onion
- 1/2 cup rosemary infusion
- Black pepper and sea salt to taste
- 1 tablespoon olive oil
- 1 cup of spinach
- 1 juiced lemon

DIRECTIONS

- Place the cucumber, tomato, garlic, onion, olive oil, spinach in a blender, season with salt and pepper and blend for 30 seconds.
- Juice the lemon, add to the blender along with rosemary infusion, and blend for another 20-seconds.
- Pour the mixture into a glass and enjoy.

Servings: 2

Alkaline Pumpkin Smoothie

A healthy, low sugar and high-fiber smoothie with pumpkin, avocado and spices. Incredibly easy to prepare and very refreshing.

- 1/2 cup of fresh pumpkin
- 1 peeled avocado
- 237 mL almond milk
- ¼ tsp vanilla
- ¼ tsp cinnamon
- 1/8 tsp nutmeg

DIRECTIONS
- Combine the pumpkin, avocado, vanilla, cinnamon, and nutmeg in a high speed blender and blend on high for about 3 minutes until a smooth consistency is achieved.
- Pour the mixture into a tall glass and enjoy.

Servings: 1

Super-Healthy Green Smoothie

This is one of the most alkalizing smoothies listed in this cookbook. So make sure you have all ingredients on hand to make it right.

- 1/2 cucumber, unpeeled, quartered
- 1/2 avocado
- 2 handfuls baby spinach, torn
- 3-4 limes, peeled (or to taste)
- 1/2 teaspoon cinnamon
- 1/2 apple, unpeeled
- 120 mL water

DIRECTIONS
- Combine the spinach, avocado, limes, cucumber, apple, cinnamon and water in a blender and pulse for a minute until smooth.
- Pour the mixture into a tall glass and enjoy

Servings: 1

Watermelon Strawberry Smoothie

A great drink for watermelon lovers, and a tasty way to cool down on hot summer days.

- 3 cups of fresh watermelon, cut in chunks
- 1 1/2 cups fresh strawberries, stems removed
- Handful of fresh mint leaves

DIRECTIONS
- Place the strawberries, mint and watermelon in a blender and pulse until smooth.
- Pour into a tall glass and enjoy.
- Enjoy.

Servings: 1

Alkaline Lime Green Smoothie

This recipe is full of fiber, vitamins and antioxidants. This can be served as a light lunch or snack.

- 1/2 cup of raw coconut meat
- 200 mL filtered water
- 2 cups spinach
- 1 medium avocado, peeled, pitted
- 1/2 medium cucumber, chopped
- 2 teaspoons lime zest, finely grated
- 2 limes, peeled, halved
- A pinch of sea salt
- A handful of ice

DIRECTIONS

- Combine the coconut, spinach, avocado, cucumber, limes and lime zest, ice and water in a high speed blender.
- Season with salt and blend until smooth.

Servings: 2

Alkaline Ginger Power Smoothie

The lime, ginger and mint pair nice with cucumber and kale in this recipe. Give a try and enjoy.

- 1 large cucumber
- 3 medium kale leaves, torn
- 4 stems fresh mint
- 4 stems fresh parsley
- 2.5 cm piece of fresh ginger
- 1 avocado
- 237 mL unsweetened coconut milk
- 200 mL of fresh lime juice
- 1-2 tsp olive oil
- 1-2 tbsp hemp seeds
- 1 teaspoon agave nectar

DIRECTIONS
- Combine all ingredients in a high power blender and blend until smooth.
- Pour into a glass and enjoy.

Servings: 1-2

Creamy Avocado Breakfast Juice

A quick and easy recipe for a wonderful alkaline balancing smoothie.

- 1 long English cucumber
- 2 stalks celery
- 1 lemon peeled
- 2 thumbs of fresh ginger or to taste
- 1 firm green pear
- 10-12 fresh spinach leaves
- 1/2 crown broccoli
- 1 avocado

DIRECTIONS
- Juice the pear and lemon and add to a blender followed by the cucumber, ginger, celery, broccoli, spinach, and avocado.
- Blend for about 2 minutes until smooth and creamy.

Servings: 2

Carrot Banana Smoothie

A nutritious and rich smoothie that is easy to make. For a sweeter taste add a little agave nectar.

- 237 mL unsweetened almond milk
- 1 tablespoon almond butter
- 1 banana
- 1/2 teaspoon cinnamon
- 3 carrots, shredded

DIRECTIONS

- Add all the ingredients to a high-speed blender and pulse until smooth and creamy.
- Enjoy.

Servings: 1

Pear and Avocado Green Smoothie

This avocado-based healthy smoothie with lemon juice and hemp seeds is a hearty way to start your day.

- 1/2 avocado
- 1 cucumber, sliced
- 1/2 lemon juice
- 2 kale leaves
- 2 dates, pitted
- 4 leaves of fresh mint
- ½ pear
- 237 mL filtered water
- 2 tablespoon hemp seeds

DIRECTIONS

- Add the avocado, cucumber, lemon juice, dates, mint, pear and hemp nuts to a blender, pour in the water and pulse until smooth.
- Pour into a glass and enjoy.

Servings: 1

Avocado Cucumber Green Smoothie

A healthy and satisfying smoothie for those who like the combination of avocado, kiwi, apple and greens.

- 1/4 cucumber,
- 1/2 handful spinach
- 1/2 avocado
- 1 celery stalk
- 2 sprigs fresh mint
- 1 kiwi, peeled
- 237 mL purified water
- 1/2 of apple

DIRECTIONS
- Pour the water into a blender.
- Slice the peeled kiwi, apple, cucumber and add to the blender, followed by the mint, avocado and celery.
- Then toss in the spinach and blend on high speed for 40 seconds until the mixture becomes smooth and creamy.
- Best to drink in the morning.

Servings: 1

Breakfast Green Smoothie

This banana-flavored green smoothie is an ideal way to get your daily dose of vitamins.

- 237 mL water
- 1 frozen banana
- 1 cup of strawberries
- 1 tablespoon olive oil
- 1/2 cup spinach

DIRECTIONS

- Add the spinach and water to a blender and pulse until smooth.
- Add the banana, berries and olive oil and blend for 20-30 seconds on high speed until the smoothie becomes creamy.
- Enjoy.

Servings: 1

Spinach Avocado Smoothie

Sweet and tasty green smoothie with grape, pear, avocado and spinach. Garnish the glass with a slice of lime and enjoy.

- 2 cups of spinach leaves, packed
- 1 ripe pear, peeled, cored, and chopped
- 15 green or red grapes
- 2 tablespoons avocado, chopped
- 1 - 2 tablespoons fresh lime juice

DIRECTIONS

- Add the lime juice and yogurt to a blender. Use them as a liquid base for blending spinach. Pulse on low speed till smooth.
- Toss in pear slices, avocado and grapes and blend for 20-30 seconds until well mixed.
- Pour into glasses and serve immediately.

Servings: 1

Carrot and Beet Smoothie

Flavorful and filling smoothie loaded with beet, carrot, red grapes and mandarin.

- 1 carrot, peeled, sliced
- 1 beet, peeled, sliced
- 1/2 cup of red grapes
- 1 mandarin, peeled
- 1 small slice of ginger, peeled
- 120 mL of water

DIRECTIONS
- Slice the peeled carrot and beet and place in a steamer basket (set over a boiling pot).
- Let steam until the vegetables are crisp and tender, about 15 minutes.
- Let cool.
- Place the mandarin, grapes, ginger, carrot and beet in a blender. Pour in the water and pulse until smooth.
- Enjoy

Servings: 1

Pomegranate Pineapple Lemon Juice

Tasty way to get plenty of nutrients and vitamins

- 1 cup chopped pineapple
- 120 mL pomegranate juice
- 350 mL water
- Juice of 1/2 lemon
- 2.5 cm piece of ginger

DIRECTIONS
- Squeeze out the juice from ½ lemon into a blender. Add the ginger, chopped pineapple and water.
- Blend until smooth.
- Pour in the pomegranate juice and pulse for 3-5 seconds.
- Pour the mixture into a tall glass and enjoy with ice.

Servings: 1

Avocado Green Smoothie

Avocado, banana and kale blended with almond milk and ginger.

- 300 mL almond milk
- 1 ripe avocado
- 1 ripe banana
- 1 sweet apple, sliced
- 1/2 large or 1 small stalk celery, chopped
- 450 mL lightly packed kale leaves or spinach
- 1 2.5 cm piece of fresh ginger, peeled
- 8 ice cubes

DIRECTIONS

- Wash the ginger. Cut the banana, apple and avocado into chunks.
- Add the milk, celery and kale to a blender and mix for 30-40 seconds until smooth.
- Add the avocado, banana, ginger, apple, and ice and blend more until the mixture becomes smooth and creamy.

Servings: 2

Powerful Green Smoothie

A healthy mixture of banana, almond milk, cucumber and strawberries. This smoothie is low fat, low sugar and high in protein, thus it can be served as a perfect nutritional snack.

- 1 1/4th cups of frozen strawberries
- 1/2 cup of cucumber, peeled, sliced
- 1 large frozen banana, broken into pieces
- 350 mL almond milk
- 1 ½ cups of kale, loosely packed, stems removed (you can also use spinach)
- Large handful of spinach (if you used kale)

DIRECTIONS

- Pour the almond milk into to a blender.
- Peel the cucumber and banana, slice into chunks and add to the milk followed by the strawberries, kale and spinach.
- Blend on high speed until smooth.
- You may add more almond milk to reach your desired consistency.
- Pour into glasses and serve immediately.

Servings: 2-3

Sweet Banana Almond Smoothie

Here is a simple and delicious smoothie recipe with almonds, agave nectar and banana. Just combine the ingredients in a blender and enjoy.

- 1 ripe banana
- 250 ml soy milk
- 1 teaspoon almonds, ground
- 1 teaspoon agave nectar

DIRECTIONS
- Place the banana, almonds, agave nectar and soymilk into a blender and pulse until a creamy and smooth consistency is achieved.
- Add more agave nectar if you like a sweeter smoothie.

Servings: 1

Tomato Avocado Rich Smoothie

This smoothie is full of fiber and antioxidants and can easily be incorporated into your healthy lifestyle.

- 1 avocado, quartered
- 1 cucumber, quartered
- 1 handful spinach leaves
- 2 tomatoes, halved
- 1/2 red pepper
- 1 lime, halved
- ½ tablespoon olive oil
- A pinch of cayenne pepper

DIRECTIONS

- Wash the cucumber, spinach, lime, tomatoes, red pepper and avocado. Cut and add to a high-speed blender.
- Add the olive oil, season with cayenne pepper and blend until smooth.
- Enjoy.

Servings: 1

Two Layer Alkaline Smoothie

Unforgettable combination of flavors in a glass.

- 2 large peeled frozen bananas
- 1 handful of spinach
- 120 mL almond milk
- 1/2 large apple
- 7 strawberries
- 1 tablespoon pumpkin seeds, ground

DIRECTIONS

- Add the banana, strawberries and almond milk to a blender and pulse until smooth.
- Pour the mixture into 2 glasses.
- Now make the second layer. Wash the blender. Blend the apple, spinach and pumpkin. Add the mixture to the top of the first layer.
- Enjoy.

. Servings: 1

Blueberry-Banana Smoothie

This creamy banana blueberry smoothie can be served as a light lunch on the go.

- 237 mL blueberries
- 1 ripe banana
- 2 cups of baby spinach
- 3 kale leaves
- 1/4 of an avocado
- 380 mL filtered water

DIRECTIONS
- Place the blueberries, banana, spinach, and kale in a blender.
- Pour in the water and pulse until a smooth and creamy consistency is reached.
- Enjoy.

Servings: 1

Mango Coconut Smoothie

Enjoy the fantastic taste of this smoothie that is full of fiber and vitamins. There's a spicy kick that creates a pretty unique experience.

- 1 cup of cucumber, chopped
- 1 large handful spinach
- 1 mango, chopped
- 237 mL coconut milk
- 1/4 jalapeno pepper, chopped
- 1 small handful of cilantro
- 3 sprigs of mint
- 1 juiced lime

DIRECTIONS

- Blend the cilantro, jalapeno pepper, mango, cucumber, spinach, mint, lime juice and coconut milk until smooth.
- Pour into a glass and enjoy.

Servings: 1

Vitamin Rich Alkaline Smoothie

This smoothie is a real arsenal of vitamins and fiber. Give a try to stay healthy.

- 450 mL almond milk or coconut milk
- 450 mL packed kale leaves
- 1 cup of frozen pear chunks
- 1 cup of frozen table grapes
- 1 small banana

DIRECTIONS

- Place the kale, pear, grapes, banana and almond milk in a high speed blender.
- Pulse for 2-3 minutes until you reach a smooth and creamy consistency.

Servings: 3

Almond Kale Banana Smoothie

A perfect breakfast smoothie. It's sweetness comes from the medjool dates, which you can ask for at your local organic grocer or order online. Add more almond milk if you prefer a thinner smoothie.

- 2 fresh bananas
- 1 tablespoon almond butter
- 237 mL almond milk
- 1/2 cup of ice
- 1 cup of kale, stems removed
- 2 medjool dates, pitted
- Shredded coconut, for garnish

DIRECTIONS

- Add the kale, dates, banana, almond milk, ice, almond butter, to a high-speed blender.
- Pulse for 60 seconds until smooth and creamy.
- Pour the mixture into a glass sprinkle with shredded coconut and enjoy.

Servings: 1

High Impact Super Green Apple Smoothie

Experience this super healthy smoothie with herbs. Feel free to add a couple of green grapes for a sweeter taste.

- 1 head of celery
- 1 cup of parsley
- 1/2 cup of pea sprouts
- 1 cup of cilantro
- 2 apples, cored, quartered
- 1 cucumber
- 2-3 large leaves of spinach
- 1 cup of dandelion greens
- 1 lemon, peeled
- 1 tablespoon ginger

DIRECTIONS
- Place the apples, cucumbers, ginger in a blender.
- Throw in the greens and herbs and blend until smooth.
- Pour the mixture into a tall glass and drink immediately.

Servings: 1

Sweet Carrot Celery and Red Pepper Smoothie

Thick, healthy and delicious. Makes a great breakfast smoothie.

- 3 small carrots, peeled
- 1 apple, cored
- 1 1/4th cups of celery, chopped
- 1 cup of red bell pepper, chopped
- 2 tbsp ginger
- 120 mL water
- 1 teaspoon agave nectar

DIRECTIONS
- Blend the carrots, apple, celery, red pepper, ginger, agave nectar and water and for 1-2 minutes until smooth.
- Enjoy.

Servings: 1

Apple Orange Green Smoothie

Make this healthy combination of greens, apple and orange into a morning ritual.

- 1/2 cup of spinach
- 1/2 apple
- 1/2 orange
- 1/2 cup of parsley
- 1 cup of celery
- 1/2 green bell pepper

DIRECTIONS
- Combine the spinach, orange, apple, green pepper, celery and parsley in a blender and pulse until smooth.
- Enjoy.

Servings: 1

Tomato Green Smoothie

A quick and healthy lunch on the go. Feel free to add tomato juice instead of water. If you like spice, add a hearty portion of cayenne and / or Tabasco sauce.

- 1 large cucumber, quartered
- 2 large tomatoes, halved
- 120 mL water
- 3 cups of kale
- Juice of 1/2 lemon,
- 1 - 2 stalks celery
- 1/2 red bell pepper, quartered
- 1/3 avocado
- Sea salt and cayenne pepper to taste

DIRECTIONS
- Add the cucumber, tomato and lemon juice to a blender and pulse for 20 seconds.
- Throw in the kale, avocado, bell pepper, pour the water and blend for another 30-40 seconds.
- Pour the mixture into a glass, season with a pinch of salt and cayenne pepper, give a stir and enjoy.

Servings: 1

Banana-Pineapple Smoothie

Sweat and healthy smoothie made with banana, pineapple, celery and orange juice,

- 4 celery stalks
- 120 mL fresh orange juice
- 1 tablespoon agave nectar
- 1 banana
- 1/2 cup of pineapple, sliced
- 1 apple, quartered
- Handful of ice

DIRECTIONS
- Juice the apple and pineapple and pour the juice into a blender.
- Add the celery, banana, agave nectar, orange juice and ice and blend until smooth.
- Enjoy.

Servings: 1

Celery Banana Smoothie with Raisins

Creamy and super healthy! The addition of raisins provides a pleasant sweetness to the smoothie.

- 2 bananas
- 2 stalks of celery
- 7-8 raisins
- 120 mL water

DIRECTIONS
- Add the bananas, celery, raisins and water to a blender and pulse until smooth and creamy.
- Pour the mixture into a glass and enjoy.

Servings: 1

Strawberry Cucumber Smoothie

This light and refreshing smoothie is a healthy combination of ingredients. The chia seeds add more nutrition to it.

- 237 mL water
- 1 cup of strawberries
- ¼ cucumber, peeled and seeded
- 1 tablespoon flaxseed oil
- 1 tablespoon chia seeds

DIRECTIONS
- Peel the cucumbers and cut into chunks. Place in a blender.
- Add the strawberries, chia seeds, flaxseed oil and water and blend to reach a smooth mixture.
- Enjoy over ice.

Servings: 1

Cherry Almond Smoothie

A heart healthy smoothie full of vitamins and minerals.

- 3 tablespoons raw almonds
- 237 mL almond milk
- 237 mL cherries (fresh or frozen)
- 1/2 teaspoon cinnamon
- 2 tablespoons agave nectar
- 1 tablespoon coconut oil

DIRECTIONS
- Place the cherries, almond milk, cinnamon, almonds, and agave nectar in a blender.
- Lastly add the coconut oil and blend until the mixture becomes smooth.
- Pour the smoothie into a tall glass, sprinkle with a dash of cinnamon and enjoy.

Servings: 1

Pear Almond Green Smoothie

An absolutely healthy smoothie. Combine all ingredients in a blender and give a try. Feel free to add other alkaline friendly fruits.

- 450 mL almond milk or coconut milk
- 1 cup spinach, tightly packed or 450 mL loosely packed
- 4 medium pears
- 1/2 cup of almonds

DIRECTIONS
- Combine the milk and spinach in a blender and pulse until the green mixture becomes smooth.
- Throw in the almonds and pears and blend on high speed until smooth.

Servings: 2

Nutty Green Smoothie

A healthy combinations of raw zucchini, cucumber, orange and nuts. It is high in protein and a good source of fiber.

- 1 orange, peeled
- 1 zucchini
- ½ cucumber, peeled
- 1/4th cup of almonds

DIRECTIONS
- Peel the zucchini, orange and cucumber, cut into quarters and place in a blender.
- Add the almonds and pulse on high speed until the mixture becomes well blended and smooth.
- Enjoy.

Servings: 1

Strawberry, Apple, Cucumber Green Smoothie

The taste of the apple and strawberries cover the taste of the spinach completely and provide a pleasant sweetness to this smoothie.

- 237 mL water
- 1 apple, cored
- 1/2 cup of cucumber, chopped
- 237 mL strawberries
- 2 tightly packed cups of spinach
- ½ lemon juice

DIRECTIONS

- Pour the water into a blender. Toss in the spinach and chopped cucumber. Blend on low speed until smooth.
- Then add the apple, strawberries, freshly squeezed lemon juice and blend on high for 30-40 seconds until smooth and creamy.

Servings: 1

Spicy Broccoli Green Smoothie

Most of your daily requirements for vegetables packed into one mega-smoothie.

- A handful of kale
- 1 big broccoli stem
- A handful of romaine
- 2 or 3 stalks of celery
- 1 large cucumber
- 1 green apple, quartered
- ½ peeled lemon, quartered
- A pinch of cayenne pepper

DIRECTIONS
- Wash the apple and cucumber, cut into quarters and add to a blender.
- Add the kale, romaine lettuce, celery, broccoli and lemon.
- Blend on high speed for a minute until a smooth consistency is reached.

Servings: 1

Coconut Citrus Smoothie

A healthy, low sugar and high-fiber smoothie that features carrots, lemon, orange and coconut milk.

- 120 mL unsweetened coconut milk
- 2 medium carrots, chopped
- ½ medium lemon, peel included
- 1 medium juiced orange

DIRECTIONS
- Peel the carrots, cut into chunks and place in a blender along with lemon slices.
- Add the coconut milk and orange juice and pulse for 30-40 seconds until smooth
- Pour into a glass and enjoy.

Servings: 1

Simple Alkaline Smoothie

The broccoli and pear gives this one a bit more of an emphasis on the alkaline theme of this book.

- 1/2 carrot, peeled
- 1/2 pear
- 1/2 cup of broccoli florets, stems removed
- 237 mL purified water

DIRECTIONS
- Peel the carrot and chop into small cubes. Place in a blender followed by the sliced pear and steamed broccoli.
- Pour in the water and blend on high speed until the mixture becomes smooth.
- Enjoy.

Servings: 1

Broccoli and Berry Morning Smoothie

A healthy combination of broccoli, almonds, strawberries and cinnamon is a real bouquet of flavors. Not to mention highly alkaline. Buy flax meal at an organic grocer.

- 10 almonds
- 1/4th cup of broccoli florets, stems cut off
- 1 cup of frozen strawberries
- 120 mL brewed green tea
- 1 teaspoon flax meal
- 1/4 teaspoon cinnamon+ for garnish

DIRECTIONS
- Combine the almonds, broccoli, strawberries, flax and cinnamon in a blender.
- Pour the green tea over the ingredients and blend on high speed until a smooth and creamy consistency is reached.
- Pour the mixture into a tall glass, sprinkle with a pinch of cinnamon and enjoy.

Servings: 1

Lemon-Lime Smoothie

This smoothie is a healthy blend of fresh greens, fruits and it is very high in vitamins C, K and A.

- 1/2 medium lemon, peeled and deseeded
- 1/2 medium lime, peeled and deseeded
- 2 medium bananas, peeled
- 1 large orange juice
- 1 3/4th cups of chopped kale or spinach
- A couple of raisins

DIRECTIONS

- Squeeze the juice of 1 orange into a blender. Add the bananas, raisins, lime and lemon and blend for 10-20 seconds.
- Lastly toss in the greens and blend for 25-30 seconds until smooth.

Servings: 1

Green Smoothie with Mango, Pineapple and Lettuce

If you are looking for a super alkaline recipe which tastes fantastic , you have already found it. Throw all ingredients in the list into a blender and enjoy.

- 2 tablespoons pumpkin seeds
- 237 mL water
- 237 mL coconut milk
- 1 cup of mango
- 1 cup of pineapple
- 1 cup of strawberries
- 1 apple, chopped
- 1/2 cup of dried apricots
- 1 cup of Romaine lettuce, chopped, tightly packed

DIRECTIONS
- Combine the greens, milk and water in a blender.
- Blend on low until the mixture becomes smooth.
- Add the apple, banana, strawberries, pumpkin seeds, dried apricots, and pineapple and blend on high speed for 1-2 minutes until the mixture is smooth and creamy.

Servings: 2

Spinach Pear Smoothie

A healthy combination of ingredients packed with fiber, protein and vitamins. Spinach gives a pleasant green color to this smoothie.

- 450 mL almond milk
- 4 medium pears
- 237 mL spinach
- 1/4th cup of almonds

DIRECTIONS
- Combine the water and spinach in a blender and blend until well mixed.
- Add the almonds, and pears and blend until the smoothie becomes creamy.
- Pour into tall glasses and enjoy with ice.

Servings: 2

Kiwi Banana Smoothie

This healthy fruit smoothie includes kiwi, banana, pineapple and water.

- 237 mL water
- 1 medium banana, sliced
- 1 cup of pineapple (fresh or canned)
- A few handfuls of ice
- 1 medium kiwi, peeled, sliced

DIRECTIONS

- Peel the kiwi and banana and slice into chunks.
- Place in a blender followed by the pineapple.
- Top with ice cubes and pulse first on low speed for 10-20 seconds, and then on high speed for additional 20 seconds.
- Pour into a glass and enjoy

Servings: 2

Green Tea Smoothie

A healthy breakfast smoothie. Unique flavor brought from the green tea.

- 450 mL kale and chard mix
- 1 1/4th cups of fresh pineapple chunks
- 1/2 avocado
- 5 cubes ice
- 1/2 orange
- 227 mL unsweetened green tea
- 150 mL water

DIRECTIONS
- Pour the green tea and water into a blender, throw in the greens and blend until smooth.
- Add the orange, avocado, pineapple and ice cubes and blend to your desired consistency.
- Pour into serving glasses and enjoy

Servings: 2

Blackberry Ginger Peach Smoothie

This is a delicious smoothie recipe that features peach, blackberries, banana and flax seeds. Ginger gives a delicate flavor to this amazing smoothie.

- 1 peach, halved
- 1 cup of blackberries
- 2 tablespoons of flax seed meal
- 1 banana
- 2 tablespoons fresh ginger (about a 2.5 cm piece if you cut it)
- 237 mL water

DIRECTIONS
- Slice the peach and banana and add to a high power blender.
- Throw in the blueberries, ginger, flax seed meal and ice.
- Pour in the water and blend until smooth and creamy.
- Pour the smoothie into 2 tall glasses and enjoy

Servings: 2

Banana Zucchini Smoothie

An ideal way to integrate raw zucchini into your healthy diet.

- 1 organic zucchini, chopped
- 1 large organic apple, cored
- 1 organic banana, peeled
- 150 mL of filtered water

DIRECTIONS

- Chop the apple, zucchini, banana and lace in a blender. Pour in the water and blend for about a minute on high until smooth.
- Enjoy.

Servings: 1

Fiery, Thai-Style Alkaline Cookbook

Southeast Asian Alkaline Recipes to Restore Your pH Level and Get You Healthy Again

FIERY, THAI-STYLE ALKALINE COOKBOOK

Southeast Asian Alkaline Recipes to Restore Your pH Level and Get You Healthy Again

ANDREA SILVER

The Southeast Asian Angle of Alkaline Cooking

If there's a single style of eating that is absolutely designed for alkalizing effects—it's the dietary habits of Southeast Asians. Large amounts of green vegetables, mushrooms, and special "super foods" like lemongrass and turmeric (curries) are incorporated naturally into the cuisine. In addition, Thai cooking in particular single-handedly kicked off the coconut-oil craze that has swept the health-food community.

Almost every recipe in this book can be made as spicy as you desire. In most Thai restaurants, there is a sliding scale of heat that you can choose, from 1 to 10—of which 10 is beyond the capabilities of an average mortal. However, during my time exploring Southeast Asia, I discovered that many of the locals possess a curious resilience to even the hottest peppers. I remember a friend eating a plate of papaya salad from the northern reaches of Isan. I took just a single bite and I had to rush to the fridge to pour some milk into my mouth. Ouch!

And let's not even get started on how powerful true, local Thai curry dishes are. Green-curries, typically served a bit like a soup with chunks of chicken and a side of rice, can be so hot that unwilling tourists often find themselves staggering from their dinner-tables in desperate attempts to cure the raging infernos in their mouths.

These types of spicy foods are of course a blessing to your diet, if you can handle them. Such foods not only keep your body alkalized, but they help you to maintain a strong immune system.

There's a special art to creating this type of food. Often the best meals in Thai or Vietnamese culture come from either street-side vendors, or inexpensive restaurants that cater to locals. The recipes I've included are a combination of some of the food I've enjoyed in such Thai cafes, as well as "fusion" cuisine that includes combinations of Western and Asian style cooking.

Some of the less healthy (but yummy) types of Thai fare I've excluded from these pages include dishes like stir-fried chicken livers with curry and rice. A recipe like that just wouldn't be very popular among my often vegan readers. If you've ever lived in Thailand (as I have), you'll discover how there is certainly a mixture of healthy foods—side-by-side with fatty, greasy, deep-fried dishes that require a bit of discipline to avoid eating too much of.

The point I'm making is that Southeast Asian cuisine does have a dark-side. A completely Thai diet, in the way locals eat—with tons of white rice and bad fats—would be a very bad idea. However, hidden in the Thai diet are those healthy gems that have become popular in the nutrition-world. These are the foods that I'm shining a light on. The less-healthy recipes you can indulge in some other time.

To dive into this cookbook, I suggest to purchase a simple wok for proper stir-frying. I also suggest to have an international grocer handy, or a good online retailer, where you can order special ingredients, including an ample supply of coconut oil, lemongrass, peppers, curry pastes, Thai crushed red chilis, and some of the other important ingredients as they appear on your culinary adventure.

With all of that being said, let's begin exploring the recipes!

Salads

Peanut Butter and Cabbage Salad

This unconventional combination actually combines two popular Southeast Asian ingredients—peanuts and soy sauce.

Ingredients

The salad:

- 1 thinly chopped head of cabbage
- ¼ head red cabbage, finely shredded
- 1 carrot, shredded
- 1 cup snow peas, finely sliced
- 5 g fresh basil leaves
- 5 g cilantro leaves
- 1 avocado, cubed
- 50 g roasted cashews, roughly chopped
- 2 tbsp black sesame seeds

Dressing:

- 2 tbsp. crunchy peanut butter

- 2 tbsp. rice vinegar
- 1 tsp. sesame oil
- 1 tsp. soy sauce
- 1 tsp. honey
- ½ tsp. hot sauce
- 1 clove garlic, minced
- 1 tsp. freshly grated ginger
- 2 tbsp alkaline water

Directions

- Combine the vegetables and avocado along with half the herbs into a large bowl.

- For the dressing, just whisk together all the ingredients and add water to thin the dressing if necessary.

- Add the hot sauce and peanut butter to the cabbage mixture and toss well together. Place into serving dish, top with the reserved herbs, cashew and the sesame seed. Drizzle the dressing on the salad just before serving.

Serves: 4-6

Spiced Mushrooms

Mushrooms are an excellent source of alkalinity.

Ingredients

- 300 g mushrooms. sliced
- Olive oil
- Salt and pepper, for seasoning
- 2 tbsp sesame oil
- 1/4 tsp white vinegar
- 2 green onions, chopped
- 1/2 slice of fresh ginger, chopped
- 1 tbsp cilantro, chopped
- Pinch of red pepper flakes (optional)
- 1 tsp toasted sesame seeds
- 1 red chili, sliced seeded

Directions

- Preheat oven to 425°.

- Roast mushrooms in the oven. Place them on a baking sheet and drizzle olive oil and sprinkle seasoning. Roast for 15 minutes until tender.

- Combine sesame oil, vinegar, onions, cilantro, ginger, red pepper flakes, and the red chili's together.

- Heat your pan on low and toss your sesame seeds in and stir until golden.

- Toss mushrooms with sauce, place on serving dish and top with toasted sesame seeds.

Old Fashioned Chinese Salad with Ginger Dressing

Ingredients

- 2 carrots, shredded
- 5 g ccilantro, chopped
- 2 cloves Garlic, chopped
- 1 tsp ginger, grounded
- 40 g green onion, chopped
- 1 mango, chopped
- 5 g mint, fresh leaves, chopped
- 1/2 small head Napa cabbage, chopped
- 150 g peanuts, roasted
- 1 pineapple, chopped
- 1 red bell pepper, chopped
- 1/2 small head Romaine lettuce, chopped
- 150 g snow peas, chopped
- 1 package noodles

- 2 tbsp honey
- 1 tbsp lime juice
- 125 g peanut butter, crunchy
- 1 peanut ginger dressing, Crunchy
- 2 tbsp soy sauce
- 1 tbsp hot sauce
- 1/4 tsp pepper
- 1/4 tsp salt
- 59 ml canola oil
- 3 tbsp rice vinegar
- 60 ml alkaline Water

Directions

- Combine the chopped ingredients: carrots, cilantro, garlic, onion, mango, mint, cabbage, pineapple, pepper, lettuce, snow peas together in a large bowl. Season with salt and pepper.

- Prepare your dressing by whisking together: Honey, lime juice, peanut butter, peanut ginger dressing, soy sauce, hot sauce and oil and water.

- Cook your noodles and add them to the chopped mixture and toss together. Place salad into serving dish and drizzle with dressing. Garnish with basil leaves.

Serves: 4

Quick-Fix Edamame with Ginger Dressing.

Ingredients

Dressing

- 3 tbsp. soy sauce
- 2 tbsp. fresh orange juice
- 1 tbsp. rice vinegar
- 1 tbsp. sesame oil
- 1 tbsp. honey
- 2 garlic cloves, chopped
- 1 tbsp. chopped ginger
- 60 ml canola oil

Salad

- 310 g shelled edamame
- 75 g red onion, cubed
- 150 g red bell pepper, cubed
- 75 g carrots, shredded
- 5 g fresh cilantro, finely chopped.
- ¼ tsp. red pepper flakes

Directions

- For the dressing: In a food blender bring together all the dressing ingredients except the canola oil. Blend until the ginger and garlic are finely minced. Slowly drizzle in the canola oil. Taste and adjust the seasonings.

- Combine all the salad ingredients in a bowl, toss well and place in serving bowl and drizzle with dressing.

Serves: 2

Spring Salad

Ingredients

- 450 g cut, cleaned greens, cut in 1-inch ribbons
- 150 g peas
- 75 g chopped fresh herbs (chives, mint, parsley)
- 4 radishes, chopped
- 1/2 avocado, diced
- 150 g green beans
- 150 g chopped sharp cheddar cubes
- 1/2 dried tomato slices
- 1/2 pickled peppers
- 7 g toasted pumpkin seeds.
- 1 cucumber, cubed
- 1/2 olives, pitted.

Dressing

- 6 tbsp. olive oil
- 3 tsp. apple cider vinegar
- 1 tbsp. fresh lemon juice
- 1 garlic clove, minced
- 3 tbsp. finely chopped shallot
- 1 tsp. dried oregano
- Pinch of sugar
- Salt and pepper (optional)

Directions

- For the dressing: Combine all the ingredients in a medium bowl and whisk.
- Place all the salad ingredients in a large bowl then drizzle with the dressing and toss. Serve immediately.

Serve: 5

Thai-Style Salad with Sesame Garlic Vinaigrette

Ingredients

- 300 g frozen shelled edamame
- 450 g baby kale, chopped
- 3 large sweet carrots, chopped
- 2 bell peppers (different colors), chopped
- 20 g cilantro leaves, chopped
- 3 green onions, chopped
- 450 g cashews

Dressing

- 78 ml canola oil
- 3 cloves garlic
- 3 tbsp. soy sauce
- 2 tbsp. alkaline water
- 2 tbsp. white distilled vinegar
- 2 tbsp. honey
- 1 tbsp. sesame oil
- 1 tbsp. ginger
- Lime juice

Directions

- Blend the dressing ingredients together in a food processor, transfer to a jar and place aside.

- In a pot of boiling water, cook your edamame for 5 minutes. Drain and allow the edamame to cool down. Combine your chopped vegetables in a large bowl.

- Mince the edamame in a food processor remove into a bowl and mince the cashews. Add the cashews and the minced edamame into the chopped vegetable mixture and toss.

- Once ready to serve drizzle the dressing over the salad and prepare into serving plates.

Serve: 6

Sweet' N Sour Alkaline Salad

A good mix of vinegar, peppers, and cilantro makes this a punch of alkaline power.

Ingredients

- 3 tbsp. fresh lemon juice
- 3 tbsp. extra virgin olive oil
- 2 tbsp. white vinegar
- 1/4 tsp salt (add more, optional)
- 1/8 tsp dill
  1/8 tsp garlic powder plus 1/2 tsp. fresh garlic, minced
- 400 g chickpeas
  10 g freshly chopped cilantro
- 1 and a half large cucumber
- 150 g green bell pepper, chopped
- 40 g onion, chopped
- 3 large carrots
- 2 tbsp. honey
- 2 tbsp. rice vinegar
- 1 tbsp. sesame seeds
- 1 tbsp. chia seeds

Directions

- Dressing: Whisk together the lemon juice, olive oil, vinegar, garlic powder, dill, salt, and minced garlic until well combined.

- Place the chickpeas, half of the cucumber and the chopped pepper in a bowl along with the onion and cilantro.

- Drizzle in the dressing over your salad.

- Next, be a little artistic and use a spiralizer to curl the cucumber and the carrots into spirals.

- Whisk the rice vinegar along with the honey and drizzle over the salad.

- Place into serving bowl and top with extra chopped cilantro along with a generous sprinkle of chia and sesame seed, you can also add nuts.

Sweet Seaweeds

Seaweed is a very common food across Southeast Asia, yet rarely consumed in the West. It's also quite alkaline and considered by some to be a "super food".

Ingredients

- 2 scallions, thinly sliced
- 1 apple
- 2 tbsp dried Wakame seaweed
- 3 tbsp. soy sauce
- 3 tbsp. rice vinegar
- 2 tbsp. Asian sesame oil
- 2tbsp. cilantro, finely chopped
- 1 tsp. sugar
- 1 tsp ginger, freshly grated
- 1/2 tsp. garlic, mined

Directions

- First soak the seaweed in water for about 5 mins. Drain and cut into wide strips.

- Whisk together sesame oil, ginger, soy sauce and sugar.

- Then slice the apples and add them along with the cilantro, seaweed and scallions.

- Toss your salad and sprinkle with sesame seeds.

Serves: 2

Chickpeas and Lemon

Ingredients

- 400 g chickpeas, boiled
- 2 tbsp dill, chopped
- 2 green chilies
- 1 tbsp. Olive oil
- 1 lemon juice
- Salt (optional)
- 1/2 tsp. black pepper
- 1/2 tsp. cumin, grounded
- Pinch of sugar

Directions

- In a pan, heat the oil and toss in the chilies along with the chickpeas for a few minutes.

- Transfer the chickpeas and chilies into a bowl and add the rest of the spices, dill and lemon juice. Toss to combine.

- Can be served with rice.

Serves: 2

Lemony Quinoa

Try spicing this one p with some Sriracha hot sauce, or a Thai chili powder.

Ingredients

- 85 g dry quinoa
- 475 ml vegetable broth
- 1 can garbanzo beans (drained and rinsed)
- 150 g cherry tomatoes cut in half
- 2 avocados, cubed
- 20 g spinach leaves
- 1 bunch of cilantro
- ½ an onion
- 2 garlic

  For the dressing:
- 2 lemons, juiced plus zest of 1 lemon
- 2 tsp mustard
- 2 tsp olive oil
- 1 tsp agave nectar
- 1/2 tsp cumin, grounded
- Pinch of salt and pepper

Directions

- First prepare your quinoa by soaking it in a pot on medium heat and adding the broth, leave for 15mins.Increase the heat to high and wait for it to boil.

- Once it boils, lower the heat to medium, allowing it to simmer. Stir for 25 mins until almost all the liquid is absorbed. Remove from the heat, cover and place it aside.

- Finely chop your cilantro and spinach and the greens and put into a bowl.

- Chop your onions and garlic and add to the spinach mixture along with the chickpeas and the cooled quinoa and mix.

- For the dressing: Just whisk all the components together and drizzle over the salad and toss. Pop in the tomatoes and avocado and toss again. Leave in the fridge for 20mins and serve.

Serves: 2

Wraps & Rolls (AKA Lunches!)

Sweet Mushroom Rolls

Ingredients

- 340g extra firm tofu
- 3 cloves garlic
- 1/2 tsp sea salt
- 1 tbsp natural brown sugar
- 2 tbsp. sunflower oil, plus extra if needed
- 240 g cups mushrooms, sliced
- butter lettuce, cilantro, mint, cucumbers, sesame seeds, (the amount is optional)
- 10 rice paper wrappers
- 2 green onions, sliced
- 3 medium shallots, sliced
- 3 tbsp ginger, grated
- 1/2 tsp sea salt
- 6 tbsp sunflower oil

Directions

- In a food processor, add the shallots, onions and ginger along with salt and mix.

- In a pan, heat your oil and add the onion mix and sauté for a few mins and remove from heat, transferring it to a bowl to cool down.

- Drain your oil and save it for later, keep the paste.

- Pat the tofu dry and cut into 6 equal chunks and arrange them into a single layer on a rimmed plate.

- In a mortar, place your sugar, salt and garlic; pound until it become a paste. Sprinkle. Adding the oil slowly while pounding. When the paste is formed, scrape it onto the slices of tofu, coating each piece.

- Cook your tofu until golden on a hot skillet over medium high heat for 5mins on each side. Remove from heat and slice the cooled tofu into pencil-thick pieces, sprinkle with salt.

- Place your mushrooms into the leftover marinade of the tofu in the pan and mix until dark in color. Transfer into a bowl.

- To make your rolls, in a large bowl comb the warm water, lettuce, ginger paste, tofu, mushrooms, cucumber, mint and seeds. In another bowl, pour hot water to dip the rice paper into.

- On a flat surface, place your dipped rice papers. Add your filling but keep it on a third of the paper, then add a bit of paste, a few lettuce leaves, cucumber, mint, seeds, cilantro and some tofu; tuck and roll the paper firmly. Arrange on serving plate.

Serves: 4

Thai-Style Quinoa Rolls

Ingredients

- 10 rice paper wraps
- 1 red pepper, sliced
- 100 g lettuce, shredded
- 150 g quinoa, cooked
- 1 large carrot, thinly sliced
- 1 avocado, sliced
- 2 tbsp creamy peanut butter
- 2 tsp soy sauce
- 1 tsp hot sauce
- 1 lime juice
- 3 tsp alkaline water

Direction

- In a bowl, dip the rice papers into hot water for a few seconds and then place on flat surface and start filling.

- In the center place some quinoa and on top add some lettuce, carrot, pepper and avocado. Wrap tightly and always fold the sides.

- To make the sauce all you have to do is whisk the soy sauce, peanut butter ,lime and hot sauce. Adding water slowly until the right consistency is formed. Serve with the rolls.

Quick Vegan Spring Rolls

The idea here is that using spring roll wrappers, you can quickly make healthy, alkalizing veggie snacks. Spring rolls are known most traditionally as a Vietnamese side-dish. You can customize them however you want, they're cheap to make, and help you to get your needed veggies every-day.

Ingredients

- Spring roll wrappers

- Combination of vegetables (sliced) such as cabbage, avocado, carrot, cucumber, tomatoes, sprouts, etc. You may add tofu, as well. Non-vegan options may include shrimp and / or chicken.

- Optional: Spice it up with Sriracha sauce or ground chili. Traditionally, such rolls are often dipped in sweet chili sauces, as well.

Direction

- Dip your wrapping paper into hot water for a few seconds. Place on flat surface and fill with the sliced vegetables. Fold the sides and wrap firmly making sure the bottom is sealed.

  Serves: depends on the amount you make.

Veggie Walnut Wraps

Ingredients

- 100 g walnuts, raw
- 2 tsp Aminos
- ½ tsp ginger, grounded
- 1 tbsp olive oil
- 1 clove garlic

To make the sauce

- 1/2 tbsp hot sauce
- 2 tbsp date syrup
- 1/4 tsp sesame seeds

Lettuce Wrap

- 3 lettuce leaves
- 2 carrots, shredded
- 1/4 red bell pepper, sliced
- Pinch of sesame seeds
- 1 stalk scallion, chopped

Directions

- Take the raw walnuts and cook them by soaking them in hot water for 10 minutes then drain.

- In a food processor, toss in the walnuts and the rest of the ingredients and blend until almost minced. Then add all the

- In each lettuce leaf, spread some off the walnut mixture and top with some pepper, shredded carrots and sesame seeds.

Serves : 3

Mango-Avocado Vegan Wraps

This is a really tasty combination of flavors for a wrap.

Ingredients

- 3 tbsp coconut oil
- 1 small onion, chopped
- 800 g cooked lentils
- 1 tbsp apple cider vinegar
- Some head butter lettuce, washed and dried
- 4 carrots, grated
- 2 avocados, sliced
- 2 mangos, sliced
- Some alfalfa, washed

Directions

- Heat coconut oil in a large pan over medium heat and add in the onions then the lentils. Add salt and pepper and vinegar. Stir for a few minutes and remove from heat

- Arrange your lettuce leaves on a plate and top each one with the lentils, carrots, mango, avocado. Sprinkle the alfalfa on top. Serve.

Serves: 4

Cauliflower Wraps

Ingredients

- 8 lettuce leaves , washed
- 1 head cauliflower, in small pieces
- 1 red onion, thinly sliced
- 1 red bell pepper, sliced
- A bit of Sriracha

For the sauce

- 2 tbsp peanut butter, crunchy
- 2 tbsp Sriracha hot sauce
- 2 tbsp almond milk
- 1 tsp toasted sesame oil
- 1/2 tsp apple cider vinegar
- 1/2 tsp turmeric

Decoration

- 1/4 cup peanuts
- cilantro
- hemp seeds

Directions

- Preheat oven to 400 degrees and bake your cauliflower in a single layer on a baking sheet and drizzle some hot sauce on it for 20mins.

- After ten minutes, shift cauliflower towards one end and add the red bell pepper and red onion to the baking sheet. Bake until cooked, but the vegetables are still fairly crunchy.

- Meanwhile, combine the hot sauce, almond milk, peanut butter, sesame oil, vinegar, and turmeric. Whisk to combine.

- Once the vegetables are ready and cool, place them in the lettuce wraps and drizzle with the sauce. Use the cilantro, peanuts and hemp seeds to garnish.

Serves: 8

Avocado Chili Wraps

A spicy, highly alkalizing blend.

Ingredients

- 1 large avocado, cubed
- 1 lime juice
- 425g chickpeas
- ½ tsp salt
- ¼ tsp cumin
- 1/2 onion, chopped
- 2 tbsp cilantro leaves, chopped
- 2 green chilis, diced
- 8 lettuce cups

Directions

- Smash the avocado with the lime juice with a fork in a bowl, then add the rest of the ingredients. Leave the lettuce cups aside.

- When desired texture is formed, add the chickpeas

- Fill each lettuce cup with avocado mixture.

Serves: 8

Lentils Wrap

Ingredients

- 1 tbsp olive oil
- 1 pepper, chopped
- 2 garlic cloves, minced
- 1 large shallot, minced
- 2 tbsp tomato paste
- 1 bay leaf
- 1 can tomato sauce
- 350 ml alkaline water
- 200 g red lentils, rinsed and drained
- 2 tbsp Thai red curry paste
- 2 tsp apple cider vinegar
- 2 tsp light brown sugar
- 1-1/2 tsp chili powder
- 1/2 tsp black pepper, freshly grounded
- 1/2 tsp kosher salt
- 1/4 tsp cayenne pepper
- 8 large lettuce leaves

Directions

- In a saucepan on medium heat, pour in the oil and add the pepper. Stir for 5 mins then add your garlic, shallots and tomato paste and stir for a minute.

- Add the rest of the ingredients, excluding the lettuce. Cover and bring to boil then reduce heat and let it simmer until the lentils are cooked and remove the bay leaf.

- In each lettuce leaf, place some of the lentils mix.

Pad Thai Wraps

Ingredients

Peanut sauce

- 125 g unsalted peanut butter
- 2 tbsp tamarind paste
- 1 tbsp soy sauce
- ½ tsp stevia extract

- 10 rice paper wrappers
- 62 g peanuts, chopped
- A bunch of cilantro
- 20 basil leaves
- Some lime wedges
- Sweet radish

Filling:

- 3 tbsp olive oil
- 1 red bell pepper, sliced
- 2 garlic cloves, crushed
- 2 eggs
- 225g firm tofu
- 1 tbsp fish sauce
- 1 tbsp tamarind paste
- ½ tsp stevia extract
- 200 g bean sprouts
- small bunch of scallions, sliced thinly
- 75 g cooked rice noodles
- 1 tsp red Thai chilies, crushed
- Soy sauce for taste

Directions

- To make the peanut sauce, mix all the ingredients in a bowl. Mix well until well combined.

- To make the filling, heat a pan on medium heat and add the oil. Toss in the peppers and cook for 10 mins. Add the garlic and eggs and mix well and quickly.

- Add the tofu, fish sauce, tamarind paste and the stevia and stir to combine for 6 mins.

- Toss in the beans, scallions, noodles and chilies and mix well. Remove from the heat and place aside.

- Prepare a large bowl full of warm water and a damp dishtowel.

- Slowly place the wrap into the warm water keeping it flat for one minute then lay on the dishtowel.

- In the centre of each wrap, divide the filling equally on each wrap. Top with the peanuts and some cilantro, basil 2 basil leaves, and a scoop of peanut sauce and a squeeze of lime.

- Fold the wraps like a burrito and arrange on serving plate.

Serves: 6

Pickled Wraps

This is a vinegar-heavy wrap that works to quickly alkalize your body.

Ingredients

- 60 ml apple cider vinegar
- 2 tbsp white vinegar
- 1 tbsp salt
- 1/2 fennel bulb, thinly sliced
- 1 small shallot, sliced
- 1 baby beet, very thinly sliced
- 2 radishes, sliced
- 80 ml buttermilk
- 80 ml plain yogurt
- 1 tbsp fresh lemon juice
- Pinch of black pepper
- 4 heads of lettuce
- 10 g cilantro leaves
- 5 g mint leaves

Directions

- Whisk together apple cider vinegar, white vinegar and 1 tbsp of salt, and ½ cup water in a large bowl. Place in the fennel: shallot, beet, and radishes and soak for 10 minutes, then drain.

- Mix the buttermilk with the yogurt and lemon juice and add salt and pepper.

- In each lettuce leaf, spoon some dressing in it and fill with the drained vegetables and add some mint and cilantro.

Serves: 8

Side Dishes

Broccoli and Tahini

Ingredients

- 4 heads broccoli florets
- 4 carrots

Sauce

- 125 ml of tahini
- 40 ml olive oil
- 150ml alkaline water
- 1 tbsp lemon juice
- 1 1/2 tsp coriander, grounded
- ¾ tsp cumin, grounded
- 1/3 tsp chili pepper, grounded
- 1 tsp of sesame seeds
- Lime slices

Directions

- Steam cook the broccoli florets for a few minutes. Place your florets in a large bowl and add the grated carrots.

- Next, prepare your sauce. Add all the ingredients in a food processor, excluding the water , sesame seeds and lime slices. Pour in half of the water and blend until the right consistency is reached, you can add more water. Place your sesame seeds and blend, then place aside.
- Pour the sauce to the broccoli mixture and toss to combine. Place in serving dish and decorate with lime slices.

Serves: 2

Zesty Brussels Sprouts

A good combination of tahini and soy will make these Brussel sprouts extra special.

Ingredients

- 10 Brussels sprouts, halved
- 1 tbsp coconut oil
- 2 tbsp tahini
- 2 tsp Soy Sauce
- 2 tbsp sesame seeds, toasted

Directions

- Cook your Brussels on steam for 10mins only.

- Once cooked drain the water, place oil in a pan and then add the Brussels and stir until golden.

- In another bowl, mix the soy sauce with the tahini, adding water until the consistency is right.

- Remove the Brussels from the pan and add the tahini and mix well, coating the sprouts.

- Place on serving dish and sprinkle with sesame seeds.

Serve: 1

Stuffed Tomatoes

Ingredients

- 2 pepper (different colors), halved
- 2 large ripe tomatoes, halved
- 2 onions, chopped
- 2 garlic cloves, crushed
- 50g blanched almonds, chopped
- 75 g of brown basmati rice, boiled and drained
- Handful of mint, roughly chopped
- Handful of parsley, roughly chopped
- 3 tbsp ground almonds
- 4 tbsp extra virgin olive oil,
- Chopped mixed herbs, to garnish
- Salt and pepper, to garnish

Directions

- Preheat the oven to 190C/Gas 5.Spoon the seeds of the halved tomatoes and roughly chop the seeds and the pulps.

- Scoop the seeds out of the peppers and brush with 1 tbsp of olive oil and place on a baking tray and bake for 15mins. Transfer to a heatproof bowl with the tomatoes and season with pepper and salt.

- Cook your rice the way you like it.

- Use the remaining oil to fry the onions for 5mins then add the garlic and the almonds and stir for a 2mins.remove from the heat and add the cooked rice, the chopped tomatoes, parsley and mint. Mix well.

- Season with salt and pepper and fill the tomatoes and peppers with this mixture.

- Arrange the stuffed tomatoes and peppers in the baking tray and pour 150ml of boiling water, uncovered for 20mins.

- Scatter with the almonds and sprinkle some olive oil. Bake until golden in color. Serve with fresh herbs.

Serve: 4

Alkalizing Greens Stir-Fry

Note: 'Aminos' are amino-acid supplements that can be added to just about any dish to fortify health effects. Give it a Google search to learn more.

Ingredients

- ½ a squash, seeds removed
- 1 onion, finely sliced
- A small piece of ginger
- 3 garlic cloves, chopped
- 1/4th a cabbage, separated
- 150 g of kale, chopped and de-stemmed
- 150 g of spinach
- 1 green chili, finely chopped
- 2 tbsp coconut oil
- 1 tbsp Thai red curry paste
- ½ a lemon, juiced
- 1 tbsp soy sauce
- Black pepper, freshly grounded
- A dash of Aminos
- A little water

Directions

- In a large frying pan, heat the coconut oil on low heat and toss in the onions and fry. After a few minutes, add the chili, ginger and garlic. Add the squash and salt. Fry until the squash is tender and make sure the garlic is not burnt.

- Toss the greens and some lemon juice along with a dash of Aminos. Season with soy sauce. Add the curry paste. Cook for a few more minutes. Remove from heat and place on serving dish.

Serves: 2

Side Dishes

Vegetable Curry

This Indian recipe requires some Garam masala, which is easy to find online or at an ethnic grocer.

Ingredients

- 1 Romanesco cauliflower
- 3 garlic cloves, chopped
- 1 onion, chopped
- 1 tbsp fresh ginger, chopped
- 75 g frozen peas, defrosted
- 1 handful parsley, chopped
- 1/2 tbsp curry powder
- 1/2 tbsp Garam masala
- 1 tsp lemon zest
- 1 tbsp olive oil
- Sea salt
- Black pepper, freshly grounded
- 1 chili, chopped (optional)

Directions

- Preheat the oven at 200 degree Celsius,

- In a large bowl, combine the onion, garlic, cauliflower then add the ginger, lemon zest, Garam masala, curry, oil, chili. Season with salt and pepper and toss.

- Place the vegetables mix into a baking tray and cook in the preheated oven for 25 mins while regularly turning.

- Transfer to serving bowl, top with peas and parsley.

Serves: 4

Brown Coconut Side Rice

Ingredients

- 370 g cups basmati rice
- 475 ml coconut milk
- 475 ml cups water
- 1/2 tsp. salt
- 2 ½ tbsp coconut, dried and shredded
- 1 tbsp coconut oil

Directions

- Brush the inside of the pot with the oil and place the rice, water, coconut milk, salt, shredded coconut and set on high heat until boiling point.

- Once it starts to boil, reduce the heat to low and leave to cook for an hour with the lid tightly shut.

- Once the rice absorbs almost all the liquid, turn the heat off and leave the pot in its place covered for 10mins.

- Serve warm as a side dish.

Serves: 4

Alkali Sushi

If you happen to be a chef who can slice exquisite sashimi; you can add raw fish to this recipe for "proper" sushi. Otherwise, enjoy this vegan recipe.

Ingredients

- 250 g brown rice
- 4 nori sheets (these are special raw, vegan sushi-wrappers).
- 1 avocado, mashed
- 1/2 cucumber, cut into thin strips
- 1/2 red capsicum, deseeded, cut into thin strips
- 50 g carrot, grated
- Aminos, to serve
- Red chili and tofu to serve (optional)

Directions

- Cook the rice the way you like. In a large bowl, place your cooked rice with a quarter of the mashed avocado and mash again.

- Your vegetables should be sliced and ready.

- Lay your nori sheets on a flat clean surface, shiny-side down. Using your wet hands, apply the rice mixture on the nori sheet (mix ¼th of the rice into half a sheet, leave a border empty 2cm wide along the edge of the sheet)

- Apply another quarter of the remaining avocado across the centre of the remaining rice. Across the avocado, arrange ¼ of the capsicum and cucumber and top with the carrot.

- Roll the sheets up firmly trapping the filling. Brush edge of nori with warm water to help the sheets to seal. Repeat the steps to roll up the other sheets. Rest your rolls once finished for 6mins.

- Slice each roll into 6 pieces and serve with Aminos and chili

Serves: 4

Lentils and Peppers

Ingredients

- 2 onions, chopped
- 2 garlic cloves, sliced
- 350g yellow peppers, seeds removed and halved
- 2 tbsp olive oil
- 250g dried red lentils, precooked
- 1 tsp dried thyme
- 400ml vegetable stock
- 4 spring onions, cut in rings
- sea salt
- Black pepper, freshly grounded
- 1 1/2 tbsp fresh lemon juice

Directions

- In a pot, heat the oil and add the chopped onions and garlic. Add the peppers, lentils, thyme and cook on low heat, covered for 9 mins.

- Then add in the onion rings, season with salt and pepper, lemon juice and cook for a further 4 mins.

- Transfer to a plate and serve.

Serves: 4

Thai Eggplant

Ingredients

The sauce:

- 4 1/2 tbsp Hoisin sauce
- 125 ml cup soy sauce
- 63 ml alkaline water
- 2 tsp chili sauce
- 2 tsp corn starch

- 1 large eggplant, sliced
- 3 bell peppers (different colors), sliced
- 1 onion, thinly sliced
- 397g firm tofu, cubed
- 2 cloves garlic, crushed
- basil leaves
- vegetable oil

Directions

- In a pan heat some vegetable oil and toss in the eggplants, then add water and stir. Turn the heat down and let the eggplants cook, constantly checking them. If the eggplants start sticking to the pan, add some water or oil.

- Once the eggplants are finished (browned), remove from heat and place aside.

- Fry the tofu in a hot pan with 2 tbsp of oil, until the liquid is gone and the tofu is golden in color. Transfer to a bowl.

- To make the sauce, whisk all the ingredients together until the cornstarch is dissolved completely. Add chili and adjust seasoning.

- In the pan add another spoonful of vegetable oil and place on medium heat. Add the onions, peppers and garlic. Cook until crispy.

- Bring together the elements: Place the tofu and vegetables in the pan with the eggplants. Adjust the heat to medium and drizzle the sauce in and stir.

- When the pan becomes hot, lower the heat and mix until the sauce thickens and coats the vegetables.

- Turn the heat off, sprinkle freshly chopped basil leaves on top, stir one more time and serve as a side dish.

Serves: 6

Spicy Brussels

Ingredients

- 400 g Brussels sprouts, halved(lengthwise)
- 3 tbsp olive oil
- 1/2 teaspoon kosher salt

For topping

- 1 tbsp vegetable oil
- 50g crushed peanuts
- 1/4 tsp cayenne pepper
- Pinch of kosher salt

For vinaigrette

- 60 ml fish sauce
- 2 tbsp alkaline water
- 2 tbsp sugar
- 1 tbsp rice vinegar
- 1 tbsp fresh lime juice
- 1 small garlic, crushed
- 1 small red chili, chopped
- 5 g cilantro, chopped
- 2 tbsp mint, chopped
- 1 tsp Sriracha sauce (optional)

Directions

- First preheat oven to 400 F.

- In a large bowl, mix the Brussels with olive oil and salt then transfer to a baking sheet and roast in the hot oven for 30 mins, turning the sides, until crisp from the outside and tender inside.

- In a pan, heat 1 tbsp of vegetable oil on high heat, add the crushed peanuts and pepper, stir for a minute until browned and season with salt and pepper. Remove from heat and set aside to cool.

- In another bowl, combine the fish sauce, water, sugar, rice, vinegar, lime juice, garlic and the chili and stir. Add the cilantro and the mint.

- Place the Brussels into a large bowl and add the fish sauce mixture and toss to combine. Top with extra Sriracha sauce for added spice.

Serves: 6

Soups and Stews

These recipes are of a more traditionally Southeast Asian style, as countries like Thailand and Vietnam are renowned for their healthy, vegetable rich soups. Loaded with greens, they are an excellent source of alkalinity and can infuse your diet with many health benefits.

Lemongrass Soup

You'll often find lemongrass as an ingredient in Asian stews. It's used to transfer flavor; but is not directly eaten. It creates a zesty, aromatic flavor in any dish that it's added to. In addition, there's a lot of research about the marvelous health benefits of it. You'll probably need to visit an Asian grocer to find a supply.

Ingredients

- 2 stalks of lemongrass
- 1 tbsp vegetable oil
- 2 garlic cloves, crushed
- 1 tsp ginger
- 960 ml vegetable broth
- 1 tsp chili paste
- 150 g shiitake mushrooms, sliced
- 75 g cherry tomatoes, halved

- 227g extra firm tofu, drained, pressed
- 5 g cilantro, chopped
- 1 tbsp lime juice
- Tamari (optional)

Directions

- Flatten the lemongrass using a large knife and pressing on them; then cut each stalk into pieces and place aside.

- In a saucepan, over medium heat, heat 2 tsp of oil and add your garlic and ginger. Fry for a 60 seconds, then add the broth along with lemongrass, chili paste, mushrooms and tomatoes. When it starts to simmer, allow the mushrooms to cook for a further 15 mins until tender.

- Cut the tofu into 1 inch cubes. In a skillet, coat with 1 tsp of oil and arrange the tofu cubes in a single layer and cook on medium heat until browned on each side, roughly 5 mins on each side.

- Transfer the tofu into the broth mix, adding the cilantro and lime juice. Season with salt and pepper and some tamari.

- Fish out the lemongrass and discard. Pour into serving bowls and serve warm.

Serves: 4

Curry Lentil Stew

Ingredients

- 1 big carrot, grated
- 1 red onion, chopped
- 1 leek, cut in rings
- 2 garlic cloves, crushed
- 1/2 tsp ginger, grated
- 1/2 tsp cumin, grounded
- 1/2 tsp chili paste or fresh chili
- 1/2 tsp turmeric
- 1 tsp curry powder
- 2 tbsp olive oil
- 250g lentils, drained
- 1.2 litres of water
- Black pepper, freshly grounded
- Sea Salt

Directions

- In a large pot, heat the oil and add the onions and fry for 5 mins. Add in the garlic, carrot, leek and cook for a few more minutes. Mix in the turmeric, chili paste, curry, and add the water and stir.

- Add the lentils to the pot and bring to a boil, then lower the heat and place the cover on and cook on low heat for 35 mins, stirring regularly.

- Once the stew is cooked, slowly blend it with a hand blender and reheat it. Season with salt and pepper. Serve warm.

Serves: 4

Lemongrass Egg Noodle Soup

Ingredients

- 160g egg noodles
- 480 ml alkaline water
- 3 lemongrass stalks, chopped
- 2 tbsp fish sauce
- 300g sliced mushrooms
- 150 shredded carrots
- 6 green onions, chopped
- 20 g fresh cilantro, chopped
- 2 tsp Hemilyan salt
- 1 tbsp red Thai curry paste
- 3 tbsp sour shrimp paste
- 3 lime juices

Directions

- In a large pot, add the water, lemongrass and the fish sauce and bring to a boil.

- Add the vegetables, the pastes, salt and the noodles and cook for 10 mins.

- Toss in the onions, lime juice and cilantro stir for a minute. Check the seasoning and adjust with salt and pepper.

- Serve warm.

  Serves: 4

Peanut Thai Stew

Ingredients

- ½ tbsp coconut oil
- 150 g onion, diced
- 5 large cloves garlic, crushed
- 200 g yams, in chunks
- ½ tsp sea salt
- 1 tsp whole coriander seeds
- ½ tsp red pepper flakes
- 1 stalk lemongrass
- 325 g zucchini, halved and sliced
- 150 g pepper, chopped in chunks
- 480 ml vegetable stock
- 180 ml water
- 400 ml light coconut milk
- 90 ml + 1-2 tbsp natural peanut butter
- 1 tbsp tamari
- 1 ½ tbsp ginger, grated
- 350g firm tofu, cubed
- 140 g fresh baby spinach leaves, loosely packed
- 2 ½ tbsp lime juice
- fresh cilantro
- lime wedges

Directions

- On medium heat, heat the oil in a pot and add the onions, garlic, yams, salt, coriander and red pepper flakes. Cover and cook for 7 mins.

- Meanwhile, cut a few slits into the lemongrass stalk and using your knife, press it open. Add the stalks, zucchini, pepper, stock, water, coconut milk, peanut butter, tamari and ginger and bring to a boil.

- Once it boils, simmer for 20 mins then add the tofu, reduce heat to low/medium-low, cover, and let simmer for 10 more minutes.

- Toss in the spinach and lime juice, adjust the seasoning. Remove the stalks and stir. Serve warm and garnish with cilantro and lime wedges.

Serves: 2

Tomato Rice soup

Ingredients

- ½ onion, chopped
- 2 garlic cloves, crushed
- 1 tsp of coconut oil
- 1 tsp ground cumin
- 85g brown basmati rice
- 2 tins of tomatoes, chopped
- 290ml yeast free vegetable stock
- small bunch parsley, coarsely chopped
- sea salt and black pepper, freshly grounded
- 4 tbsp olive oil

Ingredients

- Cook the brown rice as you like it once it is nearly cooked; in another saucepan add the prepared vegetables and cook for a few minutes.

- Add the cumin, tomatoes, the cooked rice, stock and season with salt and pepper then cook for 8 more mins.

- Transfer to serving bowl, garnish with the parsley and drizzle with olive oil.

Serves: 2

Thai Bok Choy Soup

Ingredients

- 1 tbsp coconut oil
- 1 tbsp ginger, freshly grated
- 300g mushrooms, sliced
- 1 tbsp Thai barbeque seasoning
- 1/2 tsp turmeric, grounded
- 595 ml vegetable broth
- 397g firm tofu , cubed
- 120 ml coconut milk
- Sea salt
- 5 bunches of baby bok choy , sliced

Directions

- In a pot, heat the oil on medium heat. Add half of the ginger and cook until the you can smell the flavor then add in the mushrooms and cook for 5 mins until the liquid evaporates and then add the Thai seasoning and turmeric. Stir to combine.

- Pour in the broth and add the tofu and bring to a boil. Once it boils, add the ginger and lower the heat and add the coconut milk. Stir and cook for 2 mins, season with sea salt.

- Remove from heat and add the bok choy and transfer to serving bowl, and serve hot.

Serves: 4

Spicy Thai Stew

- 1 tbsp olive oil
- 150 g chopped onion
- 150 g chopped yams
- 150 g carrots, cubed
- Sea salt
- Black pepper, freshly grounded
- 100 g chopped celery
- 4 garlic cloves, crushed
- 1/2 tsp red chili pepper, chopped
- 1 tsp coriander, grounded
- 150 g chopped red pepper
- 1 1/2 tbsp ginger, freshly grated
- 480 ml vegetable stock
- 480 ml alkaline water
- 60 g almond butter
- 3 tbsp tamari
- 2 1/2 tbsp balsamic vinegar
- 1 tsp molasses
- 65 g Swiss chard, largely chopped
- 4 tbsp fresh parsley, chopped
- 1 tsp toasted sesame oil

Directions

- In a pot, heat the oil over medium heat and add the onions, yams, carrots, salt and black pepper and stir. Cover and cook for 5 mins, then add the celery, garlic, chili, coriander, more salt, cover and cook for a further 3 mins.

- Then add in the pepper and ginger and stir. Pour in the stock, water, almond butter, tamari, vinegar, molasses and bring to a boil. Once the stew boils, allow it to simmer for a few minutes and lower the heat to low for 13 mins while stirring regularly.

- When the vegetables are cooked and tender and you're ready to serve, add in the Swiss chard, parsley and sesame oil and stir and adjust the seasoning.

Serves: 8

Cauliflower Curry Soup

Ingredients

- 1 large cauliflower, chopped
- 60 ml coconut oil
- 1 onion, diced
- 2 tbsp Thai red curry paste
- 1 tsp lemon zest
- 120 ml white vinegar
- 360 ml vegetable stock
- 1 can coconut milk
- ½ tsp sugar
- 1 tbsp rice vinegar
- Salt and pepper
- 10 g green chives, chopped
- 1 tbsp basil, freshly chopped
- Hot peppers, sliced (optional)

Directions

- Preheat oven to 400 degrees F. In a large bowl, combine the cauliflower with the coconut oil and toss to coat. Arrange the cauliflower in a single layer on a baking sheet and put in the oven and roast until golden in color, for about 25 mins.

- In a pot on medium heat, heat 1 tbsp of coconut oil and add in the onions and a pinch of salt and stir. Cook for a few minutes then add the curry paste, lemon zest and stir again. Increase the heat and add the vinegar and cook until the vinegar has evaporated.

- Place the roasted cauliflowers and half of the florets into the pot, pour in the vegetable stock and milk and add the sugar. Add all of the roasted cauliflower stems.

- Cook the soup and stir regularly, then remove from the heat and blend the soup until smooth.

- Season with salt and pepper and pour into serving a bowl. Top each serving with some cauliflower florets and a sprinkle of basil and chives and some hot pepper.

Serves: 4

Vietnamese Tamarind Soup

Ingredients

- ½ onion, cubed
- 1 tbsp olive oil
- 4 cloves garlic chopped
- 2 cups mushrooms, sliced
- 4 tomatoes, cubed
- 1 tsp sugar
- Kosher salt
- ½ tsp fresh cracked black pepper
- 950 ml vegetable stock
- 1 tsp soy sauce
- 226g firm tofu, cubed
- 1 tbsp tamarind paste
- 5 g cilantro, chopped
- 5 g chives, chopped
- Chili flakes

Directions

- In a pot, heat the oil on medium heat and add the onions and cook for a few minutes. Lower the heat and add the garlic and mushrooms and cook until tender. Then add the tomatoes, sugar, salt, pepper and cook for a further 4 mins.

- Pour the stock and soy sauce into the pot and add the tofu and tamarind. Once the soup starts to boil, simmer for 5 mins and season with salt and pepper. Serve warm.

Serves: 4

Thai Pumpkin and Coconut Soup

Ingredients

- 1 tbsp olive oil
- 1 onion, coarsely chopped
- 2 cloves garlic, crushed
- 1.5 kg butternut pumpkin, chopped
- 1 lemongrass stalk, chopped
- 1 tbsp ginger, freshly grated
- 1 bunch coriander, washed, dried and chopped
- 1 litre vegetable stock
- 400ml coconut milk

Directions

- In a large saucepan heat the oil on medium heat and add the onions and garlic and cook for a few minutes. Add the ginger, lemongrass and the roots and stalks of the coriander and cook until tender.

- Add in the pumpkin and cook for 5 more mins. Then pour the vegetable stock and bring the soup to a boil. Once it boils lower the heat and let it simmer for half an hour.

- Blend the soup until smooth and add the some of the chopped coriander and blend again.

- Add the coconut milk to the soup and pour into serving bowls. Garnish with grated coconut, coriander leaves and chili.

Serves: 8

Light Dinners

Baked Tofu with Roasted Brussels

Here's a great vegan option.

Ingredients

- 95g short grain brown basmati rice
- 675g Brussels sprouts, trimmed
- 1½ tbsp olive oil
- Sea salt
- 420g extra-firm tofu
- 1 tbsp olive oil
- 1 tbsp soy sauce
- 1 tbsp arrowroot starch
- 60 ml tamari
- 3 tbsp honey
- 2 tbsp rice vinegar
- 2 tsp sesame oil
- 2 tsp chili garlic sauce

- 2 tbsp sesame seeds, toasted
- Cilantro leaves, freshly chopped

Directions

- Preheat oven to 204 degrees Celsius. Bring a large pot of water to boil for the rice. Wash and drain the rice and place aside.

- Drain the tofu and squeeze the water out and slice into thick slabs and place on some paper towels and cover them with the towel.

- Cut the Brussels sprouts lengthways in half, add olive oil and toss to coat. Transfer to a baking sheet, arrange in a single layer and sprinkle some salt on top.

- Slice the tofu into 3 columns and 5 rows on each slab, mix with 1 tbsp of olive oil and the tamari then sprinkle the starch and toss to combine. In a baking sheet, arrange the tofu pieces in a single even layer. Place the baking sheet with the Brussels in the lower rack of the oven, and the tofu baking sheet onto the top rack and bake together for 30 mins. Bake until golden while turning halfway through.

- For the glaze, whisk 1 tsp of the chili sauce with soy sauce, honey, vinegar and sesame oil. Pour in a saucepan and bring to a boil stirring regularly, until the glaze is reduced by half, then remove from the heat.

- To serve, divide the rice into serving plates and top each serving with tofu and sprouts and drizzle with the glaze. Sprinkle the toasted seeds and cilantro.

Serves: 4

Curried quinoa with roasted cauliflower

Ingredients

- 1 head cauliflower, cut into bite-sized florets
- 2 tbsp olive oil
- ¼ tsp cayenne pepper
- Sea salt
- 2 tsp melted coconut oil
- 1 medium onion, chopped
- 1 tsp ginger, grounded
- 1 tsp turmeric, grounded
- ½ tsp curry powder
- ½ tsp cardamom, grounded
- 420 ml light coconut milk
- 120 ml water
- 190g quinoa, rinsed well in a fine mesh colander
- 115g cup raisins
- 1 tsp sea salt
- 1 tbsp apple cider vinegar
- 120g spinach leaves, chopped
- Red pepper flakes

Directions

- Preheat oven to 218 degrees Celsius. In a large bowl add the cauliflower with the olive oil, pepper and some salt and toss to combine. Arrange on a baking sheet and roast in the preheated oven for around 25 mins, until the edges are golden. Make sure you turn the florets halfway.

- In a large pot, heat the coconut oil and add the onions and cook for 5 mins, while stirring. Then add in the ginger, turmeric, curry, cardamom and stir for half a minute. Then add in the coconut milk, water, quinoa and raisins and bring to a boil.

Cook for 15 mins then remove from the heat and place aside to cool.

- Using a fork, fluff the quinoa and add in the salt, vinegar and the greens. Scoop into serving plates and top with the cauliflower and some green onions and sprinkle some red pepper flakes.

Serves: 2

Green Thai Vegetable Curry

Ingredients

- 190 g brown basmati rice, rinsed
- 2 tsp coconut oil
- 1 small white onion, chopped
- 1 tbsp fresh ginger, finely chopped
- 2 cloves garlic, crushed
- Salt
- 150 g asparagus, chopped
- 150 g carrots, chopped
- 2 tbsp Thai green curry paste
- 385 ml coconut milk
- 120 ml water
- 1½ tsps. coconut sugar
- 150g packed baby spinach, roughly chopped
- 1½ tsp rice vinegar
- 1½ tsp soy sauce
- Red pepper flakes, to garnish

Directions

- Boil the water in a large pot and add the rinsed rice and boil for half an hour, reducing the heat. Remove from the heat and drain the rice then return to the pot, cover, and place aside.

- In a large hot skillet, add a bit of oil and add the onion, ginger, garlic and some salt and stir for 5 mins. Then add in the asparagus and the carrots and cook for 3 more mins while stirring. Add the curry and cook for 3 more mins.

- Pour the coconut milk into the skillet and add 120 ml of water and 1 ½ tsp of sugar and reduce the heat and let it simmer until the vegetables are tender and cooked.

- Add the spinach to the cooked vegetables and cook until it wilts for about a minute. Stir to combine and then remove from the heat and season with vinegar and soy sauce. Scoop into serving plates and top each serving with some cilantro and red pepper flakes.

Serves: 3

Beets with Quinoa and Spinach

Ingredients

- 85 g uncooked quinoa, rinsed and drained
- 155 g frozen edamame
- 58 g slivered almonds
- 1 medium raw beet, peeled
- 1 large carrot
- 150 g packed baby spinach, roughly chopped
- 1 avocado, cubed

Sauce

- 3 tbsp apple cider vinegar
- 2 tbsp lime juice
- 2 tbsp olive oil
- 1 tbsp fresh mint, chopped
- 2 tbsp honey
- ½ to 1 tsp mustard
- ¼ tsp salt
- Black pepper, freshly grounded

Directions

- Combine the quinoa with 240 ml of water in a pot over medium heat and bring to a boil. Lower the heat and cook for 15 mins. Remove from the heat and let the quinoa rest, covered, for 5 mins, Afterward, fluff the quinoa using a fork. Place aside to cool.

- In a large pot, boil some water and add in the frozen edamame and cook for 5 mins. Drain and set aside.

- In a skillet on medium heat, toast the almonds until the edges are golden. Transfer to a bowl.

- Chop the beets and carrots. To make the sauce, just whisk all the ingredients together.

- In a large serving bowl, combine the edamame, beets, carrots, almonds, spinach, avocado and quinoa. Drizzle over the sauce and season with salt and pepper and toss to combine.

Serves: 2

Spicy, Alkalizing Stir-Fry

With both kale and Brussels sprouts, this is one of the healthiest and most alkalizing recipes in this book. Note that you can use an egg-substitute for this and make it vegan.

Ingredients

- 2 tbsp coconut oil
- 2 eggs, beaten with a dash of salt
- 2 cloves garlic, crushed
- 110 g bunch green onions, sliced
- 150 g thinly sliced vegetables, such as bell pepper, carrot or Brussels sprouts
- 1 medium bunch kale, finely chopped
- ¼ tsp sea salt
- 140 g unsweetened coconut flakes
- 325 g brown rice, cooked
- 2 tsp tamari
- 2 tsp chili garlic sauce
- 1 lime, halved
- Fresh cilantro, for garnish

Directions

- Heat a large pan and add 1 tsp of oil and pour in the eggs and cook, stirring until scrambled. Transfer to a bowl and clean the pan.

- Add 1 tbsp oil into the pan and add in the onions, garlic and the sliced vegetables of your own choice. Cook, while stirring for a minute until tender and add the kale and a pinch of salt. Stir until the kale is wilted and transfer into the egg mix.

- Add 2 tsp of oil into the pan and now pour in the coconut and cook until golden. Add in the rice and cook for 5 mins.

- Pour the egg mixture back into the pan and add the tamari and hot sauce and stir. Transfer to serving plate and squeeze lime juice on top. Garnish with cilantro leaves and lime wedges and some red pepper flakes.

Serves: 3

Traditional Pad Thai

If you have a wok instead of a skillet, I'd suggest to use it. This is an ultimate Pad Thai recipe, as good or better better than what you'll find on the streets of Bangkok.

If you lean vegetarian, simply remove the shrimp and fish sauce.

Ingredients

- 170 g rice noodles, cooked and drained
- 2 tbsp peanut oil
- 3 cloves garlic, crushed
- 2 large eggs, beaten
- 250 g small shrimp, peeled and deveined
- 360 g mung bean sprouts
- 12 g sliced scallion greens
- 60 ml rice vinegar
- 2 tbsp fish sauce
- 2 tbsp brown sugar
- 1/2 tsp crushed red pepper
- Chopped dry-roasted peanuts
- Lime wedges

Directions

- In a large skillet (or wok), heat 1 tbsp of oil, add the garlic and stir. Add the eggs and stir until scrambled. Add in the shrimps and 1 tbsp of oil and cook for 3 mins.

- Add in the noodles, bean sprouts, scallion greens, rice vinegar, fish sauce, sugar and crushed red pepper; toss to combine until well heated. Scoop into a serving bowl and sprinkle with peanuts and garnish with lime wedges.

Serves: 2

Rainbow Pad Thai

Ingredients

For the Pad Thai

- 113 g brown rice noodles, cooked and drained
- 1 zucchini
- 1 red pepper
- half a yellow onion
- 2 carrots
- 2 tbsp olive oil
- 1 egg, beaten
- 81 g peanuts, chopped
- 7 g fresh herbs

For the Sauce:

- 3 tbsp fish sauce
- 3 tbsp brown sugar
- 3 tbsp vegetable broth
- 2 tbsp white vinegar
- 1 tbsp soy sauce
- 1 tsp chili paste

Directions

- Peel the zucchini, red pepper, and onion into spirals and chop the carrots into small pieces.

- To make the sauce, place all the ingredients in a jar and shake to combine.

- In a pan, over medium heat, heat a tbsp of oil and fry the vegetables until tender. Transfer to a bowl and leave aside.

- Pour 1 tbsp of oil into the pan and add the noodles and stir for a minute. Add in the sauce and stir until it thickens and then pour in the beaten egg and let it sit for half a minute. Using tongs, toss to combine. Add in the vegetables and remove from the heat. Scoop in serving dishes and garnish with peanuts and herbs and serve.

Serves: 4

Thai Cashew Rice with Ginger Sauce

Ingredients

For the Coconut Rice:

- 320 g dry jasmine rice, soaked and drained
- 400 ml unsweetened coconut milk
- 1 clove garlic, crushed
- 1 tsp salt
- 240 ml water

For the Salad:

- 2 bell peppers, chopped
- 1 red cabbage, shredded
- 187 g shredded carrots
- 1 small red onion, finely diced
- 1 bunch cilantro, chopped
- 85 g green onions, sliced
- 1 cup cashews, finely chopped
- Spicy Thai crushed chili peppers (optional)

For the Ginger Sauce

- 91 g peanut butter
- 2 tbsp honey
- 3 tsp ginger, grated
- 2 tbsp rice vinegar
- 2 tsp sesame oil
- Water
- Lime wedges

Directions

- In a pot, mix together the rice, coconut milk, garlic, salt, and water; cover the pot and bring to a boil. Once it boils, lower the heat and simmer for half an hour. Turn off the heat and rest for 10 more minutes.

- Make the sauce, mix the peanut butter and honey and microwave for 15 seconds and then add the ginger, vinegar, oil and thin with some water and stir.

- Now fluff the rice and mix it with the chopped vegetables and cashews. Drizzle the sauce on top and serve with wedges of lime.

Serves: 8

Shirataki Pad Thai

Ingredients

- 200 g shirataki noodles, cooked
- 50 g shallots, sliced
- 1 bunch green onions, separated; whites chopped, greens diagonally sliced
- 1/2 tsp crushed red pepper
- 1 tbsp garlic, crushed
- 1 tbsp ginger, grated
- 150 g bean sprouts
- 170 g soft tofu
- 2 tbsp cilantro, chopped
- 2 tbsp peanuts, chopped
- Lime wedges

Pad Thai Sauce

- 4 tbsp wet tamarind
- 240 ml boiling water
- 1 cube mushroom bouillon
- 5 tbsp soy sauce
- 4 tbsp brown sugar
- 1 tbsp powdered peanut butter

Directions

- To make the sauce, soak the tamarind and bouillon in boiling hot water for a minimum of 15 mins. Sieve and drain and discard the stems and seeds. Add in the soy sauce, sugar, and peanut butter powder and whisk until dissolved.

- In a large pan over medium heat, add the white shallots and pepper and stir until tender. Add in the garlic, ginger, sprouts and cook for another minute. Add in the tofu and noodles and the sauce and green onions and stir. Place in serving dish and garnish with cilantro and peanuts and serve with lime wedges.

Serves: 4

Thai Quinoa Bowls

Ingredients

- 75 g broccoli, diced
- 85 g quinoa, cooked
- ½ small red onion, diced
- 40 g cup grated carrots
- Handful cilantro, chopped
- 40 g cup chopped green onions
- 2 tbsp peanuts, chopped

For the Dressing:

- 1 lime, zest and juice
- 1 tsp sesame seeds
- 1 tbsp tamari
- 1 tbsp sesame oil
- 1 tbsp rice vinegar
- 2 cloves garlic, crushed
- 2.5 cm piece of ginger, chopped

Directions

- In a large bowl mix the quinoa, broccoli, red onion and peanuts.

- Whisk the dressing ingredients and pour it on the quinoa.

- Scoop in serving bowls and serve.

    Serves: 2

Spicy, Sexy Mexican Alkaline Cookbook

Authentic Mexican Recipes to Help You Lose Weight and Feel Great, Including Vegan Recipes and Raw Recipes

SPICY, SEXY MEXICAN ALKALINE COOKBOOK

Authentic Mexican Recipes to Help You Lose Weight and Feel Great, Including Vegan Recipes and Raw Recipes

ANDREA SILVER

Getting Started With Alkaline Mexican Cuisine

Living close to the border, Mexican food is very special to me. It's a cuisine that's very hard to imitate, and whether I am in Europe or the east-coast of the United States, the further a restaurant is from Mexico, the less likely they'll get Mexican cuisine right. There's always something missing.

The trick to Mexican food is the simplicity of base ingredients. Cilantro, lime, avocado, red chili, jalapeno, tomato—the most basic Mexican ingredients tend to always be fresh, healthy, and alkaline.

There's a stereotype that Mexican food is not very healthy. In some cases, this can be true. Nico's Taco Shop (a favorite chain here in Arizona) is often loaded with lard and you're sure to pack on the pounds. If you this way all the time. However, since Mexican food at its core is quite healthy, we can see that it's not necessary to always cook with hard fats, as these types of meals evolved from Mexican street fare and their equivalents of fast-food. In reality, authentic Mexican food, with it's spicy salads and salsa Frescas, leans toward vitamin rich, alkaline, often raw healthy eating. Maybe more-so than any other ethnic cuisine in the world.

If you go to a standard Mexican restaurant in the USA, you're more likely to eat dishes that are slightly better than the greasy taco shop meals. However, there are many Mexicans in the world—and not everyone eats this way. If you happen to get invited into a home in Mexico, or you dine at a nicer establishment with a focus on regional cuisine, you're more likely to find the very healthy recipes that you will find in this book. Namely, highly alkaline, spicy, fresh meals.

By switching to a Mexican-alkaline diet, I can make some guarantees: you'll never get bored (spicy food ensures us of that), you will lose weight, you will balance your pH levels—potentially fending off deadly diseases, and you will feel full of energy.

So What's Sexy About This Cookbook?

Latin-America is unmistakably sexy, from Salsa dancing to just the whole heart and soul of the culture. You'll also notice—especially if you've ever traveled to a big city in Mexico—that both the men and the ladies are simply incredible looking. You might be wondering how they do it—and perhaps some of these recipes have finally solved that mystery.

Of course, if you really want to look your sexiest, I'd take up some dance classes to go with this kind of cooking. The very best fitness program is always something that incorporates your lifestyle. When was the last time you saw someone obese who had a labor intensive job? Almost never. Likewise, being committed to dance, yoga, running, or anything athletic is guaranteed to make you look amazing and to help you shed pounds much faster than somebody who is simply dieting or forcing themselves to go to the gym. Doubled with the recipes in this book, and you're sure to look many years younger.

With all that being said, I hope you enjoy the recipes, and that all of these peppers and spices will help you rediscover a bit of the inner-flame inside of you, waiting to be unleashed.

Soups, Appetizers and Salads

Most of my vegan-friendly recipes are allocated to this section; as Mexican cuisine provides many opportunities for vegan (as well as raw) eating in the form of soups and salads in particular. If you're not vegan and craving some dairy, virtually every recipe here can also include a bit of Monterrey or another good Mexican cheese (if it's not already included in the recipe).

Mexican Tortilla Soup

- 500 mL alkaline water
- 10 mL vegetable bouillon
- 1 large avocado, peeled and diced
- 1/2 red pepper, finely sliced
- 1 Roma tomato, diced
- 1 onion, minced
- 30 mL extra virgin olive oil
- 1/2 bunch cilantro
- 2 handfuls of spinach, rinsed and chopped
- 2 cloves garlic, minced
- 1 sprouted tortilla, sliced to strips
- 100 grams corn kernels
- 1 whole lime, sliced and quartered
- 1 jalapeño, sliced
- Salt and pepper

DIRECTIONS
- In a medium saucepan, heat 15 mL of olive oil over medium heat. Add the onion, garlic and jalapeño and cook until tender.

- Add the tomatoes, along with water and vegetable bouillon to make vegetable broth. Reduce the heat and simmer for 15-20 minutes.
- After 15 minutes, add in the chopped ingredients including spinach, corn, lime, red pepper and half of the cilantro.
- Meanwhile, in a pan, use the remaining olive oil to brown the tortilla strips.
- After cooking, ladle soup into bowls and garnish with tortillas, avocado and remaining cilantro.

Alkaline Mexican Salad

If you're not vegetarian; feel free to substitute the tofu with some organic chicken breast. Grilled slices taste the best. This salad is tasty and spicy!

- 2 wraps of sprouted tortillas
- 1/2 firm tofu, chopped
- 1 whole avocado, peeled and diced
- 1 pink grapefruit, peeled and sliced
- A handful of almonds, finely sliced
- 4 handfuls of baby spinach
- 1 whole jalapeño
- 3 Roma tomatoes
- 1/2 red onion, minced
- 1/2 lemon

DIRECTIONS
- Place tortillas over a medium bowl and push it in slightly to take the shape of the bowl. Bake tortillas in an oven at 200°C until browned and crisped. Set aside.
- Dice two of the tomatoes and set aside. Finely slice the remaining tomato and jalapeño and process in a blender until smooth.
- Mix slices of tofu, tomatoes and onions with the jalapeño mixture and place in a fridge for 10 minutes.
- Remove tofu mixture from fridge and pour into the bowl of tortillas. Mix in the almonds, avocado and grapefruit.
- Top salad with spinach and drizzle over with lemon juice.

Fresh Guacamole

So there are literally thousands of guacamole recipes out there and this is just one for a particularly healthy (and spicy) variety. Optionally for non-vegans, throw in a bit of organic mayo.

- 5 large ripe avocados, peeled, seeded and quartered
- 120 mL Roma tomatoes, finely diced
- 60 mL cilantro, chopped finely
- 30 mL white onion, minced
- 4 fresh jalapeños, finely chopped
- 2 cloves garlic, roasted
- 1 whole lemon, juiced
- Himalayan sea salt

DIRECTIONS
- In a bowl, mash avocado with garlic until smooth.
- Add the tomatoes, onions, cilantro and jalapenos and stir well.
- Cut lemon in half and drizzle juice over the mixture. Stir again.
- Add salt to taste and serve or place in a fridge until use.

Spicy Tortilla Chips

Never get stuck having to eat gross Doritos again! Learn to make your own chips using tortillas.

- 16-inch sprouted tortilla wraps
- 15 mL fresh lime juice
- 2 mL chili powder
- 1 mL cayenne pepper
- 1 mL Kosher salt
- Olive oil

DIRECTIONS
- Mix salt, chili powder, cayenne and lime juice in a small bowl and gently brush mixture over tortillas.
- Cut the tortillas into 8 small wedges. Arrange wedges in a single layer on a baking pan greased with olive oil.
- Bake at 400 degrees for around 8 minutes until chips are golden brown and crispy.
- Remove baking pan from oven and cool. Cut into smaller strips if desired.

Alkalized Refried Beans

Optionally, replace the can of pinto beans by preparing whole, fresh pinto beans—although this takes more time. There are many refried beans recipes in Mexico, and this is just one.

- 1 can pinto beans
- 1 medium onion, chopped
- 2 fresh jalapenos, chopped
- 2 cloves garlic, minced
- 15 mL extra virgin olive oil
- 30 mL chopped fresh cilantro
- 5 mL chili powder
- 250 mL water
- salt and pepper, to taste
- 120 mL shredded cheddar cheese

DIRECTIONS
- Heat olive oil in a pan over medium heat. Saute onions until tender. Add chopped jalapenos halfway through if you want them to be crispier.
- Mix in garlic and chili powder and cook for about 1 minute more.
- Pour in water and bring mixture to boil until most of the water has been removed.
- Coarsely mash beans using spoon or spatula.
- Remove from pan and season with salt and pepper.
- Pour in the grated cheese while hot, adjusting taste by adding more salt and pepper.
- Stir in the cilantro, remove beans from pan and serve.

Mexican Sauteed Greens

A great side-dish with just about anything.

- 15 mL extra-virgin olive oil
- 1/2 onion, minced
- 1 jalapeno, sliced finely
- 250 mL cherry tomatoes, halved
- 200 grams kale
- 80 mL fresh cilantro
- 200 grams baby spinach
- Himalayan sea salt and ground pepper
- 15 mL fresh lemon juice

DIRECTIONS

- Heat olive oil over medium heat in a pan. Stir in the onion and jalapeño and saute for 2-3 minutes until onion is tender and translucent.
- Stir in tomatoes and cook for another 2 minutes.
- Add the kale, cilantro and spinach and sprinkle with salt and black pepper. Cook and stir until greens are wilted.
- Drizzle over with lemon juice and adjust taste with salt and pepper.
- Serve and enjoy.

Andrea's Basic Pico de Gallo Recipe

A basic but addicting recipe for the Mexican relish that tastes great on everything—it's also highly alkalizing.

- 1 kg ripe plum tomatoes
- 1 large white onion
- 3 jalapeños
- 35 mL fresh cilantro
- 20 mL lime juice
- 10 ml lemon juice
- Himalayan sea salt

DIRECTIONS
- Chop tomatoes, onion and jalapeños finely.
- Mix veggies well in a bowl.
- Add lime, lemon juice, salt and cilantro and adjust salt to taste.

Alkaline Mexican Green Sauce

This can be served by itself or used as a dip. It's kind-of like a cross between a smoothie, guacamole, and a soup. It's also both raw and vegan.

- 700 mL fresh baby spinach
- 250 mL zucchini
- 1 large avocado, chopped
- 250 mL chopped fresh cilantro
- 60 mL chopped celery
- 250 mL red bell pepper
- 60 mL chopped red onion
- 30 mL fresh lime juice
- 4 cloves garlic
- 1 jalapeño, minced
- 5 mL Mexican seasoning
- Himalayan sea salt, to taste
- 250 mL alkaline water

DIRECTIONS
- Pour all ingredients into a food processor and puree for 1-2 minutes until the desired smooth consistency is achieved. Set aside some tomato and cilantro.
- Add more salt, chili, and seasonings to taste.
- Garnish with remaining tomato and cilantro.
- Serve hot or place in a fridge.

Mexican Broccoli Salad

A special, spicy salad recipe. Feel free to put the dressing on any other type of salad that your heart desires.

- 450 grams finely chopped broccoli
- 350 mL chopped Roma tomatoes
- 1 cucumber, chopped
- 120 mL toasted pumpkin seeds

Dressing

- 2 avocados, peeled and seeded
- 60 mL fresh lime juice
- 2 cloves garlic, minced
- 1 jalapeño, seeds removed and minced
- 100 mL chopped cilantro
- 5 mL cumin
- 10 mL Himalayan sea salt

DIRECTIONS
- Blender all dressing ingredients until pureed. Place puree in a salad bowl and set aside.
- Add chopped broccoli, cucumber and tomatoes to the dressing in the bowl.
- Mix together with the pumpkin seeds, serve and enjoy.

Fiesta Verde Alkaline Soup

Another tasty and completely raw and vegan soup-slash-dip to enjoy.

- 720 mL fresh baby spinach
- 1 small zucchini, chopped
- 1 large avocado, chopped
- 250 mL chopped cilantro
- 1 rib celery, chopped
- 220 mL chopped red bell pepper
- 60 mL minced red onion
- 1 lime, juiced
- 3 cloves garlic, chopped
- 1/2 jalapeño, seeded
- 5 mL Spice Hunter Salt Free Mexican seasoning
- 5 mL Himalayan sea salt
- 250 mL alkaline water
- Tomato, for garnish

DIRECTIONS
- Put all ingredients in a blender and puree until smooth for around 60 seconds. Set aside around a quarter of cilantro for garnish.
- Adjust consistency by adding more water.
- Adjust taste using salt, pepper and Mexican seasoning.
- Garnish with chopped tomato and remaining cilantro and serve.

Corn and Poblano Chile Sauté

- 30 mL olive oil
- 2 poblano peppers, seeded and chopped
- 1 medium red onion, chopped
- 300 mL thawed frozen corn
- 2 cloves garlic, chopped
- salt and pepper, to taste
- 30 mL fresh lime juice

DIRECTIONS

- Heat olive oil in a pan over medium-high heat.
- Add the chopped poblano pepper and onions and cook for around 5 minutes, stirring often.
- Add the corn, garlic, some salt, and a dash of black pepper and cook, stirring often, until the corn is heated.
- Drizzle over the lime juice, remove heat and serve warm.

Monterey Mexican Beans

- 150 mL refried beans
- 4 mL fresh lime juice
- 60 mL mild salsa
- kosher salt
- 80 mL grated Monterey Jack cheese
- 1/4 avocado, diced

DIRECTIONS
- In a bowl, combine the beans, lime juice, half of the salsa, and a pinch of salt.
- Sprinkle grated cheese on top and place bowl for 1 minute in an oven hot enough to melt the cheese.
- Top bowl with dices of avocado and pour the remaining salsa.
- Serve with spicy tortilla chips.

Avocado Salad With Toasted Cumin Dressing

It's strange how well cumin and avocado go together. This heart-healthy recipe is full of good omega acids.

- 4 large ripe tomatoes, chopped
- 2 large ripe avocados, seeded, peeled, and chopped
- 1 large red onion, mincedd
- 400 mL arugula leaves
- 5 mL cumin
- 75 mL chopped cilantro

Toasted Cumin Dressing

Fresh, full of cumin, and great on salads of even sandwiches. Vegan-friendly, but you can make it "not so vegan friendly" by creaming it with some organic mayo.

- 60 mL fresh lime juice
- 25 mL apple cider vinegar
- 15 mL honey
- 20 mL cumin seeds, lightly toasted
- 75 mL chopped fresh cilantro leaves
- 65 mL olive oil
- 65 mL canola oil
- Salt and fresh ground pepper

DIRECTIONS
- To make the dressing, thoroughly mix the lime juice, vinegar, honey, cumin, and cilantro in a bowl.
- Gradually whisk in the oils and sprinkle with some salt and a dash of pepper. Set aside.

- In a large bowl, gently mix the tomatoes, avocados, onions, arugula leaves and cumin dressing.
- Adjust taste by adding more salt and pepper if desired.
- Sprinkle ground cumin and chopped cilantro over salad and serve right away.

Alkaline Black Bean Salad

For a non-vegan version, add some sour cream. It also tastes good with red or green tabasco sauce.

- 50 mL apple cider vinegar
- 30 mL fresh lime juice
- 15 mL honey
- 5 mL ground cumin
- 80 mL extra virgin olive oil
- Kosher salt and freshly ground black pepper
- 1/2 small ripe mango, peeled and diced
- 1/2 yellow bell pepper, diced
- 400 mL cooked black beans
- 1 jalapeno, seeded and minced
- 1 red onion, minced
- 80 mL fresh cilantro leaves, chopped

DIRECTIONS

- In a bowl, mix the vinegar, lime juice, honey and cumin.
- Gently whisk in the oil until emulsified.
- Sprinkle with salt and pepper to taste and set aside.
- Mix the mango, pepper, beans, jalapeno and onion together in a separate bowl.
- Drizzle the vinegar mixture over the salad and toss to combine.
- Season the salad with salt and pepper and garnish with chopped cilantro.

Jalapeno-Alkaline Slaw

This type of spicy coleslaw is a lot better tasting (in my opinion) than regular coleslaw recipes, as normally slaw is a kind of mediocre dish.

Dressing

- 30 mL soy sauce
- 2 small limes, juiced
- 15 mL toasted sesame oil
- 15 mL honey
- 1 small dried jalapeño, cut into rings
- 5 mL salt
- 5 mL freshly ground black pepper

Salad

- 450 mL shredded peeled jicama
- 3 medium raw beets, peeled and shredded
- 1 cucumber, peeled, seeded, and thinly sliced

DIRECTIONS
- To make the dressing, simply mix the soy sauce, lime juice, sesame oil, sugar, chile, salt and pepper in a bowl.
- In a large salad bowl, combine the jicama, beets, and cucumber, pour in dressing mixture and toss to combine.
- Cover and place in a fridge.
- Serve cold.

Green Tomato Salad

- 2 large tomatoes
- 1 red onion, thinly sliced
- 1 serrano chili, thinly sliced
- 15 mL chopped cilantro leaves
- 5 mL Mexican oregano
- 15 mL extra-virgin olive oil
- 10 mL apple cider vinegar
- Salt and pepper

DIRECTIONS
- Slice tomatoes into thin pieces and arrange them on a plate with the sliced onions.
- Evenly spread the chilies alongside the tomatoes and sprinkle the cilantro on top and around the plate.
- In a mixing bowl, combine and thoroughly mix the oregano, oil, and vinegar.
- Drizzle the vinegar mixture on top of salad just before serving.
- Season with salt and pepper to taste.

Black Bean Soup With Kale and Cilantro

If you're not vegan, top it with some sour cream.

- 250 mL salsa
- 1 pinch allspice
- 900 mL cooked cans black beans
- 750 mL low-sodium chicken broth
- 200 mL chopped cilantro
- 200 mL chopped kale

DIRECTIONS
- In a large saucepan, mix the salsa and allspice and cook over medium heat for about 3 minutes.
- Stir in the black beans and broth, raise heat to medium-high and bring mixture to a boil.
- Lower the heat to simmer 10 minutes then use an immersion blender or potato masher to coarsely mash the beans in the pot.
- Remove heat, ladle soup into serving bowls and garnish with fresh greens of kale and cilantro.

Mexican Salad With Lime Dressing

Another great, fresh salad. You can spice it up by adding jalapenos, habaneros or other peppers.

- 1 large head Romaine Lettuce, chopped
- 250 mLCherry tomatoes, halved
- 1 avocado, diced
- 1/2 cucumber, sliced
- 1/2 small yellow onion, thinly sliced
- 120 mL corn kernels
- 1/3 bunch fresh cilantro

Lime Dressing

- 80 mL extra virgin olive oil
- Juice of 2 medium limes
- 2 mL tabasco sauce, or to taste
- 2 mL sea salt
- 1 mL black pepper, freshly ground

DIRECTIONS
- Mix all salad dressing ingredients and shake or thoroughly whisk them together to combine. Set aside.
- Chop all salad ingredients and mix together in a large salad bowl.
- Drizzle the top with as much salad dressing as desired. Mix well and enjoy.

Alkaline Mexican Grilled Corn

- 2 ears corn, shucked and chopped into 6 pieces
- 1 mL extra-virgin olive oil
- kosher salt and black pepper
- 100 mL chopped fresh cilantro
- 8 mL fresh lime juice and lime wedges for garnish

DIRECTIONS
- Heat grill to medium.
- In a medium bowl, mix corn with the oil and salt and pepper.
- Grill corn, uncovered, until tender for 10 to 12 minutes.
- Place the grilled corn to the serving bowl and sprinkle with the cilantro and drizzle lime juice.
- Serve corn with lime wedges.

Tomatillo Salsa

- 450 grams tomatillos, husked, washed, and quartered
- 2 garlic cloves, peeled
- 1/2 sweet white onion
- 1 jalapeno pepper, seeded and chopped
- 25 mL fresh lime juice
- 30 mL chopped fresh cilantro

DIRECTIONS

- Add the garlic in a blender and process until chopped.
- Mix in the tomatillos, onion, jalapeño, and lime juice and process until fairly smooth.
- Stir in the cilantro and season with salt and pepper.
- Cover and store in a fridge until use, or serve with a main course meal right away.

Cheesy Grilled Jalapeños

This recipe is a bit less vegan the others in this section, but I couldn't resist adding it. Stuffed jalapenos have been a mainstay in my home ever since I first learned to make them. If you want a pure vegan version, try stuffing with walnuts, or a mixture of spices within some eggless mayo.

- 200 mL shredded soft goat cheese
- 120 mL reduced-fat cream cheese, softened
- 120 mL grated parmesan cheese
- 120 mL minced seeded tomato
- 30 mL thinly sliced green onions
- 15 mL chopped fresh sage
- 2 mL kosher salt
- 16 jalapeno peppers, halved vertically and seeded
- Cooking spray
- 30 mL chopped fresh cilantro

DIRECTIONS
- Preheat grill to medium-high heat.
- Combine cheeses, tomatoes, onions, sage and salt in a bowl, stirring well.
- Stuff cheese mixture into the halved peppers and flatten top.
- Place peppers, cheese side up, on grill rack coated with cooking spray.
- Grill for about 5 minutes until bottom of peppers char and cheese mixture lightly browns.
- Remove peppers from grill and serve sprinkled with cilantro.

Mexican Pumpkin Soup

A combination of spicy and lightly sweet creates a gourmet side-soup.

- 2 carrots, chopped
- 1/2 onion, diced
- 2 cloves of garlic, minced
- 250 mL pumpkin puree
- 120 mL cup cooked quinoa
- 2 mL cinnamon
- 2 mL chili powder
- 2 mL smoked paprika
- 1 mL cayenne pepper
- 350 mL vegetable stock
- 250 mL water
- 250 mL coconut milk
- Zest and juice of 1 lime
- Salt and pepper
- Extra-virgin olive oil

DIRECTIONS
- Heat some oil over medium-high heat in a saucepan.
- Stir in the onions, garlic and carrots and cook for about 5 minutes until they begin to soften.
- Add the spices and cook for about 2 more minutes.
- Add the chicken stock, water, lime zest and juice, and pumpkin puree and bring to a boil.
- Simmer uncovered for between 15 to 20 minutes until the soup has thickened to desired consistency.
- Add the quinoa and cook for 5 more minutes.
- Using an immersion blender, blend the soup until most solids liquefy.
- Return soup to the pot and add milk.

- Season with salt and pepper and serve

Main Courses

Many of these alkaline entrees do require cheese to complete, because cheese is such an essential part of Mexican cuisine. However, if you are vegan, quite a few of the cheesy ingredients can be substituted with a bit of creativity.

Mexican Tofu Manicotti

- 1 pack firm tofu, sliced
- 450 grams refried beans
- 15 mL chili powder
- 15 mL oregano
- 250 grams manicotti shells
- 600 mL water
- 450 grams picante sauce
- 450 grams sour cream
- 240 mL shredded monterey jack cheese
- 60 mL sliced ripe olives
- extra virgin olive oil

DIRECTIONS

- In a bowl, mix tofu with beans, chili powder, and oregano.
- Stuff mixture into uncooked manicotti shells.
- Arrange manicotti shells in a baking pan greased with olive oil.
- Mix the water with picante sauce and pour over the stuffed manicotti shells in the baking pan. Cover and cool in a fridge for 8 hours.
- Remove baking pan from fridge at least 30 minutes before baking.
- Cover and bake at 350°C for 50-55 minutes.
- Uncover, spoon sour cream over the top and sprinkle with cheese, onions and olives.
- Bake for 5-10 minutes more until cheese is well-melted.

Mexican Wild Rice

- 340 grams ripe Roma tomatoes, cored
- 1 white onion, chopped
- 3 jalapeños, chopped
- 480 grams wild rice
- 80 mL extra virgin olive oil
- 4 cloves garlic, minced
- 7.5 mL sea salt
- 400 mL frozen corn
- 120 mL minced fresh cilantro
- 1 whole lime

DIRECTIONS

- Place, in order and without stirring, the rice, water, tomatoes, garlic, onion, jalapeños and corn into rice cooker. Set to cook.
- Once cooked, open lid and gently mix rice to spread ingredients.
- Drizzle with olive oil and lime and season with salt and pepper.
- Add in the minced cilantro, stir well and serve. Makes 8 servings.

Alkaline Enchiladas With Lettuce and Cheese

- 15 mL extra virgin olive oil
- 2 onions, chopped
- 2 cloves garlic, minced
- 250 mL zucchini, finely chopped
- 1 red bell pepper, chopped
- 2 handfuls spinach, chopped
- 1 can black beans, drained and rinsed
- 600 mL enchilada sauce
- 15 mL nutritional yeast
- 7.5 mL ground cumin
- 25 mL fresh lime juice
- 2.5 mL Himalayan sea salt
- 2.5 mL garlic powder
- 5 mL chili powder
- 4 whole wheat tortilla wraps
- 1/2 head iceberg lettuce
- 400 grams Monterey jack cheese, shredded
- Apple cider vinegar
- Minced spring onions and chopped cilantro, to garnish

DIRECTIONS
- Preheat oven to 350°F.
- In a pot, heat olive oil over medium-low heat. Sauté chopped onions until translucent.
- Add the garlic, reduce heat and continue cooking for 1-2 minute more.
- Add bell pepper, zucchini, black beans, and chopped spinach. Cook for around 7 minutes on medium-low heat.

- Stir in the enchilada sauce, along with nutritional yeast, cumin, lime juice, salt, garlic powder and chili powder. Adjust according to taste.
- Take around 200 mL of the mixture and evenly spread out in a thin layer over the bottom of the baking pan.
- Take around 150 mL each of the mixture and stuff them into each tortilla before wrapping.
- Wrap the tortillas with the folded side facing down and arrange them over the baking pan. Pour remaining mixture over the tortillas and sprinkle with jack cheese.
- Bake tortillas at 350°F for around 20 minutes. Remove from oven when cooked.
- Garnish enchiladas with spring onion and cilantro and serve alongside lettuce dressed with salt and apple cider vinegar. Makes 4 servings.

Alkaline Bean Quesadillas

- 120 mL sour cream
- 60 mL shredded Feta cheese
- 60 mL tomato salsa
- 4 sprouted grain tortillas, 40-inch
- 250 mL frozen corn kernel
- 120 mL black beans, drained and rinsed
- 2 spring onions
- Olive oil

DIRECTIONS
- Thoroughly mix sour cream, Feta cheese and salsa in a bowl.
- Divide mixture into four parts and spread on each tortillas.
- Also divide the corn, beans and onions into four parts and stuff each part into each of the tortillas before folding them in half.
- Grease frying pan with olive oil and preheat over medium heat. Cook each of the tortillas on the pan, flipping and cooking the other side once the other side is browned until the cheese melts.
- Remove from the pan and serve in wedges.

Alkaline Mexican Mozzarella Pizza

- 450 grams vegan refried beans
- 15 mL olive oil
- 6 large sprouted tortillas
- 120 mL enchilada sauce
- 140 mL shredded mozzarella
- 250 mL chopped black olives
- 2 stalks green onion, chopped
- 1 Roma tomato, chopped

DIRECTIONS

- Heat beans in a medium-sized saucepan.
- Meanwhile, heat the oil in a frying pan and heat both sides of the tortillas for less than a minute until golden brown.
- Remove beans from heat and spread over one tortilla and sandwich with another tortilla.
- Spread enchilada sauce at the top and sprinkle with shredded mozzarella cheese.
- Heat pizza in an oven until the cheese is melted. Top it with black olives, green onions, and tomatoes.
- Cut into quarters and serve.

Garlic and Cheese Quesadillas

- 2 cloves garlic, unpeeled
- 20 mL olive oil
- Salt and pepper, to taste
- 320 mL grated Monterey jack cheese
- 150 mL finely grated Parmigiano Reggiano
- 200 mL fresh goat cheese
- 10-inch sprouted tortillas
- 500 mL water

DIRECTIONS
- Pre-heat oven to 200°F.
- In a saucepan, bring water to boil over medium-high heat. Add the garlic cloves and cook until tender for 4-6 minutes. Drain, let cool, peel, and place in a small bowl.
- Using a fork, mash the garlic to make a garlic paste, add olive oil and adjust taste using salt and pepper.
- In a bowl, mix together the Monterey Jack, Parmigiano Reggiano, and goat cheese.
- Brush the garlic mixture over one side of each tortilla and place tortillas on a tray with the greased side facing down.
- Spread the cheese mixture over the tortillas, covering only half the surface and leaving 1-inch bare on the edge.
- Fold the tortillas in half, enclosing the cheese.
- In a pan, cook two of the quesadillas covered over medium heat for around 4 minutes. Uncover and flip after one side is browned. Cook until other side is brown and cheese I well-melted.
- Serve warm.

Alkaline Mexican-Style Lasagna

- 12 small sprouted tortillas
- 1 yellow onion, chopped
- 1 green bell pepper, chopped
- 100 grams baby spinach
- 1 head broccoli
- 1 yellow crooked neck squash, chopped
- 1 zucchini, chopped
- 2 chives, chopped
- 250 mL black beans
- 250 mL red enchilada sauce
- 1 jar marinara sauce
- 450 mL black olives
- 5 mL cumin
- guacamole

DIRECTIONS

- Preheat oven to 400 degrees.
- Mix spinach, broccoli, squash and zucchini and soak them in alkaline water for at least an hour. Drain.
- Grease baking pan with olive oil, and line a layer of 6 tortillas. Set aside.
- Mix enchilada sauce, marinara sauce and cumin together in a large bowl.
- Mix together drained veggies, bell pepper and black beans in a separate bowl
- Spread a layer of veggie bean mixture on top of the tortillas and cover with sauce.
- Place a layer of tortillas and another layer of veggies and sauce over the top.
- Top with olives and bake in oven for around an hour. Do not overcook.
- Spread chopped chives and fresh guacamole over the top after removing dish from oven.

- Serve and enjoy.

Healthy Alkaline Tacos

- 120 mL walnuts
- 120 mL raw blanched slivered almonds
- 120 mL chopped dried tomatoes
- 30 mL extra virgin olive oil
- 7.5 mL ground cumin
- 1 mL garlic powder
- 1 mL onion powder
- 1 mL chili powder
- 10 mL Bragg liquid aminos
- 2 mL Himalayan sea salt
- 15 mL chopped fresh parsley
- Romaine Lettuce, shredded
- Pico de Gallo

DIRECTIONS
- To make the filling, blend walnuts and almonds in a blender and process until well-ground.
- Mix in the sun-dried tomatoes, olive oil, spices, liquid aminos, salt, and parsley and pulse until well-mixed. Adjust taste using salt or aminos.
- Stuff the nut mixture into shreds of Romaine lettuce, along with the spice and tomato mixture.
- Stuff in Pico de Gallo into the lettuce and top with your preferred alkaline cream or dressing.
- Serve and enjoy.

Green Salad With Queso Fresca and Spicy Tortillas

- 500 mL vegetable oil
- 4 small spicy tortillas (see recipe), halved and cut crosswise into strips
- 15 mL apple cider or white wine vinegar
- 45 mL extra virgin olive oil
- 2 mL salt
- 2 mL black pepper
- 400 grams watercress, thick stems removed
- 450 mL chopped cherry tomatoes
- 250 mL Queso Fresca

DIRECTIONS
- Heat olive oil on a medium-sized frying pan, then fry tortilla strips until browned.
- Transfer tortillas to paper towels to drain and sprinkle with salt.
- Thoroughly mix vinegar, salt, and pepper in a small bowl, add olive oil and whisk until well-blended.
- Toss watercress with vinegar mixture in a large bowl and divide among 8 serving plates.
- Divide tomatoes and tortilla strips among salads and sprinkle with cheese.

Alkaline Chimichangas

- 30 mL extra virgin olive oil
- 500 mL chopped and cooked vegan beef or chicken
- 1 yellow onion, minced
- 1/2 red bell pepper, finely diced
- 2 garlic cloves, finely minced
- 1 Roma tomato, chopped
- 120 mL chopped green chilies
- 2.5 mL salt, or to taste
- Fresh ground black Pepper, to taste
- 7.5 mL dried Mexican oregano
- 5 mL chili powder
- 2 mL ground cumin
- 10 mL nutritional yeast
- 30 mL minced fresh cilantro
- 4 large sprouted tortillas
- olive oil for deep-fry
- 30 mL shredded Monterey jack cheese

DIRECTIONS
- Blend onion, pepper, and garlic until finely chopped in a blender.
- In a pan, heat oil over medium heat. Saute onion, garlic and pepper mixture for 5 minutes.
- Mix in the tomatoes, chilies and cook until the onion softens.
- Sprinkle salt and black pepper, oregano, chili powder, cumin, and cilantro and cooking for 2 to 3 more minutes.
- Once veggies are cooked, stir in the chopped vegan meat and nutritional yeast. Saute for for a few minutes until meat is heated and yeast mixes well with the veggies. Remove heat.

- Divide the vegan meat mixture into four and spread each over each of the tortillas and top with jack cheese.
- Fold the tortillas, enclosing the filling. Deep-fry each Chimichanga in olive oil about half an inch deep, flipping until both sides are crispy and brown.
- Remove oil by placing the Chimichangas on a paper towel.
- Serve with a dollop of guacamole, sour cream or salsa and alongside chopped tomatoes and lettuce if desired.

Meatless Green Burrito

- 2 burrito-size sprouted grain tortillas
- 140 mL cooked black beans
- 120 mL cooked wild rice
- 150 mL chopped Romaine lettuce
- 1 Roma tomato, diced
- Fresh guacamole
- 1/4 red onions, minced
- 150 mL fresh cilantro
- Salt and pepper, to taste
- 150 mL Monterey jack cheese

DIRECTIONS
- Soak lettuce, tomatoes and cilantro in alkaline water for 10 minutes. Drain and set aside.
- Brown each side of tortillas by heating over open flame.
- In a pan over low heat, mix cooked rice, lettuce, beans an tomato for 1-2 minutes. Add salt and pepper to taste.
- Stuff in rice mixture into the tortillas and top with cilantro, guacamole and cheese.
- Fold into a wrap and enjoy.

Quinoa Brown Burrito

- 120 mL cooked Quinoa
- 80 mL cooked black beans
- 1 sprouted tortilla
- 1 lime, juiced
- 5 mL extra virgin olive oil
- 1/2 chopped avocado, peeled and seeded
- 80 mL chopped kale
- 80 mL chopped spinach
- 80 mL chopped lettuce
- 1/2 Roma tomato
- 1/4 spring onions, chopped
- 1 clove garlic, minced
- 5 mL ground cumin seeds
- 5 mL chili powder
- 2 sprigs cilantro
- Saslt and pepper, to taste

DIRECTIONS
- In a pot, mix beans with just enough water and add cumin, chili powder, garlic and salt.
- Cook for 10 minutes over medium heat until most of the water is gone.
- Lay sprouted tortilla flat on a plate and add the quinoa, beans, onion and tomato, cilantro and avocado.
- Drizzle with fresh lime over the top and sprinkle with salt and pepper to taste.
- Top with mixed kale, spinach and lettuce and roll into a wrap.

Spicy and Cheesy Bean Tacos

Ugh, so good!

- 450 mL cooked black beans
- 15 mL olive oil
- 125 mL minced white onion
- 2 cloves garlic, minced
- 1 can roasted tomatoes
- 100 mL canned diced green chilis
- 5 mL chili powder
- 1 mL garlic powder
- 1 mL red pepper flakes
- 1 mL dried oregano
- 1 mL paprika
- 2 mL cumin
- Salt and pepper to taste

Spicy Cashew Cheese Dip

Can also serve with corn chips, or whatever you prefer.

- 250 mL raw cashews
- 1 lime, juice and zest
- 30 mL nutritional yeast
- 4 mL kosher salt
- 5 mL chile powder
- 2.5 mL ground coriander
- 2.5 mL ground cumin
- 2.5 mL garlic powder
- 8 soft taco shells
- Monterey jack cheese to top

DIRECTIONS
- Soak cashews in enough water and drain. Place cashews along with other spicy cheese ingredients and puree until smooth. Set aside in a fridge.
- In a large pan, heat olive oil over medium-high heat.
- Stir in minced onion and cook until soft for around 5 minutes, followed by the spices, salt, pepper and minced garlic and continue cooking until fragrant.
- Stir in the black beans, tomatoes and green chilis.
- Reduce heat to medium and cook for 3- 5 minutes until warm.
- Divide mixture and stuff each portion into taco shells topped with spicy cashew cheese.
- Serve immediately.

Broccoli and Sprouts A La Mexicana

- 200 grams chopped broccoli

- 120 grams Brussels sprouts
- 30 mL extra virgin olive oil
- 1/2 spring onion, minced
- 2 jalapeños, finely chopped
- 2 medium Roma tomatoes, chopped
- 5 mL sea salt

DIRECTIONS
- Heat olive oil in a pan and sauté chopped onions and jalapeños until soft.
- Add chopped tomatoes and sprinkle with salt. Stir until tomatoes are well-cooked and mushy.
- Mix in the chopped broccoli and Brussels sprouts.
- Cook for around 5-10 minutes until desired tenderness of broccoli I achieved. Serve as a side-dish or inside tortillas as tacos.

Huevos Rancheros

A famous Mexican breakfast. If you feel motivated to cook in the mornings, where's one way to start your day.

- 35 mL olive oil
- 1 onion , peeled and finely sliced
- 2 cloves garlic, minced
- 2 red peppers , deseeded and finely sliced
- 2 fresh red chilies , deseeded and finely sliced
- 1 dried chilli
- 3 fresh bay leaves
- salt and pepper, to taste
- 2 x 400 g tins of chopped tomatoes
- 2 large tomatoes , sliced
- 6 large eggs
- 6 tortillas
- 150 g Cheddar cheese , to serve

DIRECTIONS
- In a pan, heat the olive oil over high heat.
- Mix in onions, garlic, pepper, chilies, bay leaves and some salt and pepper.
- Cook, stirring often, for 10-15 minutes until caramelized.
- Stir in tins of chopped tomatoes and use back part of spatula to flatten and mash them.
- Bring to boil then lower heat and cook for 5 more minutes.
- Sprinkle more salt and pepper to adust taste.
- Lay sliced tomatoes over the top of the mixture, then using a spoon, make small holes or wells in the thick tomato stew and crack in the eggs.
- Create at least 6 wells, one for each egg.
- Cover and cook for another 3-4 minutes.

- Meanwhile, heat the tortillas using a separate pan, 20 seconds for each side.
- After cooking, serve tomato stew with warmed tortillas, sprinkled with grated cheddar. Spoon tomato stew into the tortillas, wrap and enjoy.

Alkaline Mushroom Tacos

Mushrooms are packed with alkaline properties. In combination with peppers, it's a real alkaline infusion.

- 400 mL fresh mushrooms, chopped
- 1/2 medium white onion, diced
- 1 jalapeño, seeded and finely chopped
- 180 mL water
- 1/2 small lime, juiced
- 30 mL extra virgin olive oil
- 15-ounce canned tomatoes
- 2 garlic cloves, peeled and coarsely chopped
- salt

DIRECTIONS

- In a saucepan, combine the mushrooms, onion, chili, water, lime juice and lard or other fat. Bring to a boil over medium-high heat, covered for 2-4 minutes.
- Uncover and cook until all water is gone and mushrooms begin to fry in fat.
- While the mushrooms are cooking, mix tomato with the garlic and puree in a blender.
- When the mushrooms begin to fry, pour in tomato puree and cook until thick.
- Season with salt and put into a serving bowl. Serve with tortillas on the side if desired.

Mexican-Stuffed Mushrooms

- 4 portabella mushrooms
- 1 poblano chili
- 120 mL tomato salsa
- 2 fresh jalapeno, seeded and sliced
- 480 mL Queso Anejo
- 60 mL chopped cilantro
- olive oil

DIRECTIONS
- Roast poblano chili in a broiler until blackened. Place in a bowl and remove skin and seeds. Dice and set aside.
- Preheat oven to 375°F.
- Scrape out darks areas in mushroom and clean them by rinsing in water.
- Lay a sheet of foil flat on a baking pan an grease with olive oil. Place mushrooms with gill side up.
- Spread around 30 mL of salsa over each mushroom.
- Divide chopped poblanos and divide over each mushroom.
- Sprinkle with sliced jalapeños and top each with around 120 mL of Queso Anejo cheese.
- Bake for around 20 minutess until mushroom are tender.
- Garnish with fresh cilantro and serve.

Shiitake and Mozzarella Quesadillas

- 15 mL extra virgin olive oil
- 15 mL low-sodium butter
- 120 mL minced white onions
- 1 jalapeño, chopped
- 2 garlic cloves, finely chopped
- 450 grams shiitake mushrooms thinly sliced
- 30 mL chopped fresh epazote leaves
- 10 mL Kosher salt, to taste
- 250 mL grated Mozzarella cheese
- Sprouted tortillas
- Tomato salsa

DIRECTIONS
- Pre-heat oil and butter in a medium-sized pan over high heat.
- When butter begins to sizzle, mix in white onion and saute until soft and translucent, usually for around 3 to 4 minutes.
- Add jalape and minced garlic and cook for about a minute until fragrant.
- Pour in the mushrooms and cook for around 5 minutes, stirring often.
- Allow the juices of mushrooms to come out and dry up before mixing the epazote leaves and salt. Stir well and cook for 1 more minute. Do not overcook.
- Brown the tortillas on dry skillet over medium heat for about 20 seconds each side.
- Place 1-2 tablespoons of the mushroom mixture and 1-2 tablespoons of grated mozzarella on each of the tortillas. Spread, covering only 1/2 of the tortilla.
- Fold to half moon shape and press.
- Cook for 1-2 minutes each side until cheese is well-melted.
- Serve immediately.

Main Courses

Spicy Chili Relleno Casserole

- 2 (7 ounce) cans whole green chile peppers, drained
- 1/2 jalapeño, seeded and minced
- 250 mL shredded Monterey Jack cheese
- 250 mL shredded Cheddar cheese
- 2 eggs, beaten
- 150 mL evaporated milk
- 40 mL whole wheat flour
- 4 mL oregano flakes
- 4 mL cumin
- 250 mL canned tomato sauce
- olive oil

DIRECTIONS

- Preheat oven to 175°C. Grease a baking pan with olive oil.
- Lay around half of the chilies evenly on the baking dish.
- Mix the two cheeses along with the minced jalapeños, oregano and cumin.
- Take half of cheese mixture and sprinkle over the chilie in the baking pan and top with remaining chilies.
- In a bowl, thoroughly mix together the eggs, milk, and flour, and pour over the top of the chilies.
- Bake mixture in the preheated oven for around 25 minutes.
- Remove relleno from oven, cover with tomato sauce, and resume baking for 15 more minutes.
- Sprinkle with remaining spicy cheese mixture while hot an serve.

Calabaza Chipotle Chili With Avocado

- 30 mL olive oil
- 1 medium red onion, chopped
- 2 red bell peppers, chopped
- 650 grams calabaza, peeled and cubed
- 4 garlic cloves, minced
- 15 mL chili powder
- 10 mL chopped chipotle pepper in adobo sauce
- 5 mL ground cumin
- 2 mL ground cinnamon
- 1 bay leaf
- 750 mL cooked black beans
- 400 mL canned diced tomatoes, undrained
- 450 mL canned vegetable broth
- Kosher salt, to taste
- 2 avocados, diced
- 3 sprouted tortillas or spicy tortilla chips (see recipe)
- Cilantro for garnish

DIRECTIONS

- Heat olive oil in a medium stockpot. Stir in the onion, bell pepper and calabaza and cook, until the onions become translucent.
- Lower heat to medium-low and mix in the garlic, chili powder, chopped chipotle peppers, cumin and cinnamon.
- Cook, stirred, for 30 seconds, until fragrant. Add the bay leaf, black beans, tomatoes aong with its liquid and vegetable broth. Stir well and cover for about 1 hour, stirring from time to time.
- Check to see if calabaza is tender enough and water has reduced to yield good consistency. Add salt to taste and remove heat.

- Slice tortillas into strips aan fry them in olive oil for 4-7 minutes, stirring occasionally. Drain in paper towels.
- Serve the calabaza chili in serving bowls, topped with crispy tortilla strips and garnished with diced avocado and chopped cilantro.

Alkaline Breakfast Tacos

- 10 mL olive oil
- 1 small white onion, diced
- 3 garlic cloves, minced
- 1 small zucchini, sliced into thin strips
- 1 small yellow squash, sliced into thin strips
- 1 red pepper, seeded, membranes removed and chopped
- 1/2 lime, juiced
- Salt
- Pinch red pepper flakes
- Fresh cilantro for garnish
- Tomato salsa
- 6 small sprouted tortillas

For Scrambled Eggs

- 6 eggs, scrambled
- Hot sauce
- Salt and freshly ground black pepper
- 1 tomato, chopped

DIRECTIONS
- Heat olive oil in a skillet over medium heat. Stir in onions along with a dash of salt.
- Cook for about 5 minutes until the onions are softened and turn translucent.
- Stir in garlic and a pinch of red pepper flakes , and cook for 30 seconds more.
- Add the zucchini, yellow squash and bell pepper. Cook for 5-minutes, stirring often, until the squash is softened and cooked.

- Remove heat and drizzle lime juice over the veggies. Season to taste with salt, stir and set aside.
- Mix eggs in a bowl with some hot sauce, a sprinkling of black pepper and a pinch of salt.
- Scramble egg mixture over medium-low heat until the eggs are mildly cooked. Mix in the tomatoes and cook for a few seconds more, then transfer to a bowl.
- Warm tortillas in a pan and transfer each to a plate. Top each with scrambled eggs, veggies, and garnish with jalapeño, feta and cilantro.
- Top with tomato salsa and serve warm.

Chili Tempeh Picadillo

- 30 mL olive oil
- 1 small onion, finely chopped
- 1 red pepper, diced
- 1 clove garlic, minced
- 1 green chili, de-seeded and minced
- 5 mL ground cumin
- 4 mL oregano flakes
- A dash of cinnamon
- 2.5 mL salt
- 240 grams Tempeh
- 400 grams canned chopped tomatoes
- 30 mL tomato paste
- 7 mL apple cider vinegar
- 60 mL raisins
- 60 mL pitted green olive, halveds

DIRECTIONS
- Warm oil in a pan over medium heat. Stir in onions and pepper. Sauté for about 5-8 minutes until soft.
- Add garlic, chili, spices and salt and cook for 3 more minutes.
- Crumble the tempeh into the pan using your hands.
- Mix in the remaining ingredients, except the olives, and stir well.
- Cover pan and simmer for 10-15 minutes until thick but saucy.
- Stir through the olives and cook for another minute. Season and serve.

Green Cilantro Rice

- 80 mL chopped cilantro
- 80 mL chopped kale
- 3 cloves garlic
- 1 serrano chili, seeded and halved
- 800 mL low-sodium chicken broth
- 15 mL extra virgin olive oil
- 120 mL yellow onion, mince
- 500 mL long-grain white rice
- 15 mL kosher salt

DIRECTIONS

- Mix together cilantro, kale, garlic, chili, and 500 mL broth in a blender and puree until smooth. Set aside.
- Heat olive oil in a pan over medium-high heat. Add the onion and cook for 1-2 minutes until softened.
- Stir in rice and sprinkle salt. Cook for about 2 minutes until rice turns opaque.
- Pour the cilantro mixture and the remaining broth into the rice and stir.
- Bring mixture to a boil then lower heat to simmer.
- Cover and cook for 10-15 minutes until rice is tender.
- Remove heat and serve.

Potato and Bean Nachos

- 10 mL extra-virgin olive oil
- 250 mL chopped red onion
- 2 cloves garlic, minced
- 1 red sweet pepper, diced
- 450 mL canned black beans, drained and rinsed
- 10 mL ground cumin
- 5 mL chili powder
- Fine sea salt, to taste

Potato Wedges

- 2 medium Russet potatoes, sliced into wedges
- 15 mL grapeseed oil
- Sea salt and freshly ground black pepper
- Chili powder, to taste

DIRECTIONS
- Pre-heat the oven to 425°F.
- Rinse and drain potatoes without peeling.
- Arrange potatoes on a greased baking pan and toss potatoes with oil. Season with sea salt, pepper, and some chili powder.
- Place fries in preheated oven and bake for about 15 minutes. Flip and roast for 15 to 18 more minutes until lightly golden brown.
- While potato is being baked, in a large skillet over medium heat, sauté the onion, garlic, and pepper in the oil for about 8 minutes until the onion turns translucent.
- Add the black beans, cumin, chili powder and salt to taste and saute for 5 more minutes.
- Set aside until ready to use. Reheat before serving.
- Serve beans on top of potatoes and top with salsa, guacamole or pico de gallo.

Sweet Potato Nachos

This is really a three-part recipe, and is a good vegan alternative to some of the other main dishes. You'll find the cashew 'dressing' has a unique, nutty goodness when paired with the sweet potato fries.

- 4 large sweet potatoes
- 30 mL extra virgin olive oil
- Salt and fresh ground black pepper, to taste

Lime-Black Bean-Corn-Sweet Onion Hash

- 1 ear corn
- 1 can black beans
- 1/2 medium sweet onion, minced
- Juice and zest of 1 lime
- Salt and ground black pepper, to taste

Cashew Cream

- 250 mL raw cashews
- 1 lemon, juiced
- 30 mL nutritional yeast
- 60 mL water
- 1 medium tomato, chopped
- cilantro, chopped

DIRECTIONS
- Preheat oven to 400°F.
- Thinly slice the sweet potatoes and place on a baking pan.
- Top potatoes with the oil, salt, and pepper and cook for about 45 minutes until crispy.

- Meanwhile, mix all hash ingredients in a pan and cook over medium heat for about 30 minutes. Remove heat and set aside.
- Mix all cashew cream ingredients in a blender and puree until smooth.
- Serve nachos on a plate along with cashew cream dip.

Pepper and Mushroom Fajitas

- 1 poblano pepper, seeded and thinly sliced
- 2 bell peppers, seeded and thinly sliced
- 1 jalapeño, seeded and thinly sliced
- 1 yellow onion, cut into thin rings
- 4 portobello mushrooms, stems removed, wiped clean and thinly sliced
- 2 ripe avocados
- juice of 1/2 lime
- sea salt, cumin & garlic powder
- 6 small flour or corn tortillas
- Cilantro, to garnish

DIRECTIONS

- Heat a large skillet and a medium skillet over medium-high heat and heat olive oil to the large skillet, then the onion and peppers. Sprinkle with enough salt, cumin and garlic powder.
- Cook until softened and slightly caramelized, stirring often. Remove heat, cover and set aside.
- Meanwhile, add a dash of oil to the medium pan, then add the mushrooms.
- Sprinkle with a bit of salt and once softened and brown. Remove from heat, set aside and cover.
- Prepare guacamole by combining the two avocados with the juice of half a lime and a generous pinch of salt.
- Warm tortillas in the microwave or oven and you're ready to go.
- Serve tortillas with mushrooms, guacamole and chopped cilantro.

Avocado and Lime Mexican Rice

- 1 liter hot cooked brown rice
- 1 ripe avocado, seeded and peeled
- 30 mL fresh lime juice
- 2.5 mL kosher salt
- 1 mL ground cumin
- 60 mL chopped cilantro leaves

DIRECTIONS
- In a bowl, scoop out flesh of avocado and mash with lime juice, salt, and cumin.
- Add rice and cilantro until well mixed.
- Adjust salt and lime to taste.
- Serve and enjoy!

Red Mexican Rice

- 30 mL extra-virgin olive oil
- 6 scallions, sliced, green and white parts segregated
- 2 cloves garlic, chopped
- 500 mL raw long-grain white rice
- 600 mL low-sodium chicken broth
- 530 mL tomato sauce
- 2 mL chili powder
- kosher salt and black pepper, to taste

DIRECTIONS

- In a large saucepan, heat the oil over medium-high heat. Stir in the scallion whites and garlic and cook for 1-2 minutes until softened.
- Add the rice and cook, stirring often, until grains are opaque.
- Add the broth, tomato sauce, chili powder, somee salt, and pepper and stir to combine.
- Bring to a simmer, cover and cook for about half an hour until the rice is tender.
- Remove heat and let the rice stand, covered, for about 5 minutes.
- Mixs with a fork and sprinkle with scallion greens before serving.

A Message from Andrea

Thank you so much for taking the time to read this book. I hope that this was of some benefit to you.

You can find many more books like this one I've created by checking out my Amazon page at the following address: http://www.amazon.com/Andrea-Silver/e/B00W820AR6/.

You can also get in touch with me personally at AndreaSilverWellness@gmail.com if you have any questions or ideas.

Until next time.

Andrea

37311426R00158

Printed in Great Britain
by Amazon